Inn-to-Inn
Walking Guide

Virginia & West Virginia

Copyright © 2001 by Su Clauson-Wicker
Printed in the United States of America
Published by Menasha Ridge Press
First edition, first printing

Distributed by The Globe Pequot Press

Library of Congress Cataloging-in-Publication Data

Inn-to-Inn walking guide, Virginia and West Virginia/by Su Clauson-Wicker.
        p.   cm.
    Includes index.
    ISBN 0-89732-338-6 (pbk.)
    1. Walking--Virginia--Guidebooks.
2. Walking--West Virginia--Guidebooks.
3. Bed and breakfast accommodations--Virginia--Directories.
4. Bed and breakfast accommodations--West Virginia--Directories.
5. Virginia--Guidebooks.
6. West Virginia--Guidebooks.
I. Title.
GV199.42.V82 C53 2001
796.51'09755--dc21

                                        00-068361
                                            CIP

Cover design by Grant Tatum
Cover photo © by Su Clauson-Wicker
Photo Credits:
    Skip Brown, p.13
    David Fattaleh, WV Division of Tourism, p. 21
    Steve Shaluta Jr., WV Division of Tourism, pp. 28, 29, 34, 55, 65, 70

Menasha Ridge Press
P.O. Box 43673
Birmingham, Alabama 35243
www.menasharidge.com

Inn-to-Inn
Walking Guide

Virginia & West Virginia

by Su Clauson-Wicker

Menasha Ridge Press ❖ Birmingham, Alabama

In memory of my father, Bob Clauson, for whose untimely death these rambles through the eternal beauty of nature seemed to be preparing me. Dad, may you continue to walk in timeless beauty.

This book is also dedicated to my husband Bruce Wicker, the best hiking partner of them all.

Contents

Inn-to-Inn Legend

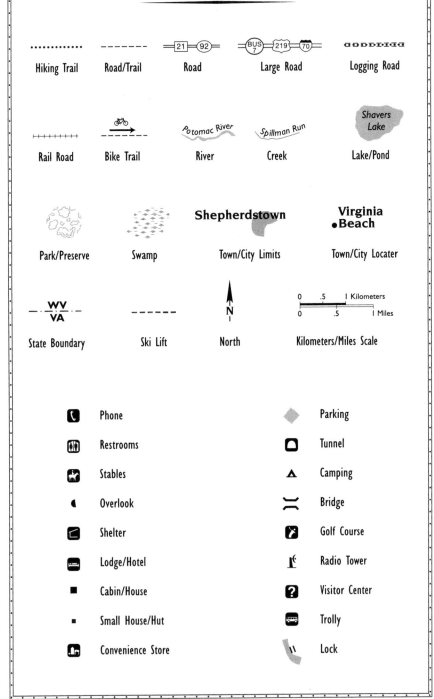

Hiking Trail   Road/Trail   Road   Large Road   Logging Road

Rail Road   Bike Trail   River   Creek   Lake/Pond

Shavers Lake

Park/Preserve   Swamp   Town/City Limits   Town/City Locater

Shepherdstown

Virginia
•Beach

WV / VA
State Boundary   Ski Lift   North   Kilometers/Miles Scale

📞	Phone	◆	Parking
🚻	Restrooms	▢	Tunnel
🏇	Stables	▲	Camping
◖	Overlook	⤫	Bridge
◤	Shelter		Golf Course
🏨	Lodge/Hotel		Radio Tower
■	Cabin/House	❓	Visitor Center
▪	Small House/Hut	🚋	Trolly
🏪	Convenience Store		Lock

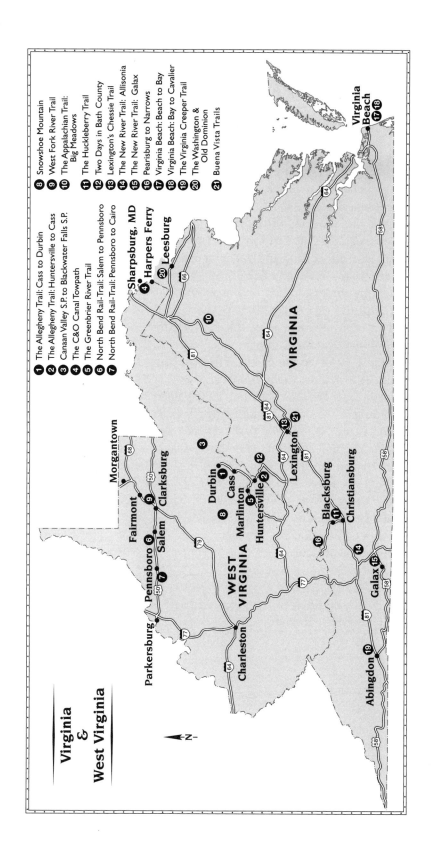

Virginia & West Virginia

- **1** The Allegheny Trail: Cass to Durbin
- **2** The Allegheny Trail: Huntersville to Cass
- **3** Canaan Valley S.P. to Blackwater Falls S.P.
- **4** The C&O Canal Towpath
- **5** The Greenbrier River Trail
- **6** North Bend Rail-Trail: Salem to Pennsboro
- **7** North Bend Rail-Trail: Pennsboro to Cairo
- **8** Snowshoe Mountain
- **9** West Fork River Trail
- **10** The Appalachian Trail: Big Meadows
- **11** The Huckleberry Trail
- **12** Two Days in Bath County
- **13** Lexington's Chessie Trail
- **14** The New River Trail: Allisonia
- **15** The New River Trail: Galax
- **16** Pearisburg to Narrows
- **17** Virginia Beach: Beach to Bay
- **18** Virginia Beach: Bay to Cavalier
- **19** The Virginia Creeper Trail
- **20** The Washington & Old Dominion
- **21** Buena Vista Trails

Acknowledgments

You don't hike almost 300 miles in two states without a little help and advice from a lot of people.

I am particularly grateful to my mother-in-law Betty B. Bobo, my aunt Shirley Verbanic Cochrane, and my good friends Susan Kwilecki and Laurie Zuckerman for their support and encouragement of my plans to disappear into the semi-wilds for several seasons.

And special thanks to my friend Nancy Chapman for her superhuman efforts with editing and encouragement.

I also thank my many friends and acquaintances who helped me to broaden my understanding and experience of the trails of Virginia and West Virginia, especially Tony O'Leary, Betty Carver, Steve Shaluta, David Fattaleh, and the West Virginia Department of Tourism; Gil and Mary Willis; Jeannie Dunham; Karl Frischkorn; Steve Drummheller; Erwin and Carol Asam of the Bavarian Inn, Leslee McCarty of the Current B&B; Randy Stemple, Mark Abbott, D. J. Allen, and the rest of the North Bend Trail Association; Mike Valach and Joe Stevens of Snowshoe Mountain; George and Kathy Sprowls; Tracy Asbury of Allegheny Outdoor Center; John and Kathy Panek; Carter Acona; Pam and Ron Stidham; Yvonne Emerson; Jean Tardy Clark of the Lexington Visitors Center; Don and Chipper Holt; Shawn Hash of Tangent Outfitters; Karita Knisely; New River Inn Coffee Club; Virginia Beach Convention and Visitors Center; Voncile Gilbreath of Barker, Campbell, Farley, and Mansfield; Jane Johnson of Virginia Beach Resort; Cindi Brooks of the Abingdon Convention and Visitors Bureau; Jim Goode; Jim and Nathalie Graham; Pam McMurray of Norris House; Joe Turzanski and Charles Garratt.

Also, thanks to Bud Zehmer, an editor who knows how to give a writer a little freedom but who insists that she give clear directions for those who want to follow.

Su Clauson-Wicker

Introduction

This is the hiking book for people who like to walk but don't necessarily like to carry big packs and sleep on the ground at night. This book offers a change of pace for those who backpack. If you could walk for days but you like a shower, a good meal, and a warm bed at the end of the trail; if you think longingly of rambles in the British Isles from one bed-and-breakfast to the next; if you like to pamper yourself at least once in a while, these hikes are for you.

Hiking from inn to inn is easy. All I carried for these one- to two-day trips was water, lunch, a change of underwear, a few emergency supplies, and my credit card. Unencumbered, I traipsed farther and faster than other hikers bowed over by huge packs and weighted down by heavy footgear. I was free to stop and explore my surroundings without having to worry about what would become of the substitute home on my back. I made better time and enjoyed leisurely dinners in lodging that often held more comforts than home.

This book includes hikes that meander through America's cultural landscape past living history sites and museums, as well as those that traverse West Virginia and Virginia's remote mountaintops. Several hikes lead through extensive resort holdings before joining public forest trails; others travel public rights-of-way over private lands. One hike ends in the boreal environment of West Virginia's highest forest, another at Virginia Beach's Boardwalk, and another at a shopping mall. All these hikes are about exploration, both external and internal.

If you aren't a regular walker but are reasonably fit, you can probably do a 10- to 15-mile hike on a flat rail-trail. But you will enjoy it more if you aren't distracted by your tender feet or your creaking joints. You'll find more pleasure in the rhythmic pace of your hike if you get in shape by walking at least 30 minutes every other day for several weeks. You also can test whether your shoes will be comfortable over the long haul and what clothes work best. My husband and I learned that running shoes rather than hiking boots made for easier walking on most trails, and that we should never, ever substitute clammy, cotton socks for polypropylene. Ditto for cotton shirts—if you get sweaty and wet, you stay that way. Synthetic materials work better, especially in cool weather when losing body heat can be dangerous.

Why Walk?

The main benefit of training walks is that you could become addicted to walking for life. According to Aaron Sussman, co-author of *The Magic of Walking:*

"Walking is the exercise that needs no gym. It is the prescription without medicine, the weight control without diet, the cosmetic that is sold in no drugstore. It is the tranquilizer without a pill, the therapy without a psychoanalyst, the fountain of youth that is no legend."

Walking is also an aid to clear and creative thought, and a preventive for cancer, osteoporosis, diabetes, and other diseases.

"If the body be feeble, the mind will not be strong. The sovereign invigorator of the body is exercise, and of all the exercises walking is the best," said Thomas Jefferson more than 200 years ago. Scientists are again emphasizing the mind-body connection, suggesting that muscles in action keep the brain awake and that activity drains away emotions, leaving the mind free to think.

The thinking walk has a long and distinguished history, beginning with Aristotle's Peripatetic School of philosophy. Robert Louis Stevenson, Thomas Edison, Charles Dickens, Abraham Lincoln, and Albert Einstein were just a few of the world's great minds who did their best cogitating on foot. Sigmund Freud did not only his thinking but also had many of his discussions while trotting along the streets of Vienna with students in tow. Jean-Jacques Rousseau wrote of walking: "Never have I thought so much; never have I realized my own existence so much; never have I been so alive."

Even more magical than the thinking walk is the walk to escape thinking, the walk during which you put a problem aside and come back with a solution. When the natural, rhythmic action of the body takes over, the intuitive mind can fly free to work at unconscious levels.

Walking brings us back to our senses of sight, smell, touch, hearing, and the feeling of being an individual. We bind our lives together, and we nod hello to fellow pedestrians. No road rage on the trail. "I never knew a man to go for an honest day's walk for whatever distance . . . and not have his reward in the repossession of the soul," wrote George Trevalyan, the British historian.

Walking is Good Medicine

Walking may save your life, provided it is regular. Because humans are upright animals, our hearts must work against the pull of gravity to keep blood flowing through nearly 100,000 miles of circulatory byways every 24 hours. When we walk, the muscles of our feet, calves, thighs, buttocks, abdomen, and diaphragm contract and release rhythmically, squeezing the veins and pressing the blood along. They act almost like a second heart.

When we are sedentary, our blood tends to pool in our bellies so our hearts must work harder to keep a limited supply of blood moving to our organs. When we walk, our circulation speeds up and our heart rate and blood pressure go down. As we continue to work our muscles over time, dormant blood vessels open up and our ability to process oxygen is increased.

Brisk walking burns 350 to 500 calories an hour; it offers built-in weight control. If you do it aerobically, walking raises your level of beta-endorphins—the feel-good hormones. If you keep up the pace for 20 to 30 minutes, you'll walk yourself into an exercise high.

Walking encourages bone growth, a big plus in avoiding osteoporosis, and, if you clock 15-minute miles, you encourage your body to secrete more growth hormone, which strengthens bones even more. There's even talk that women who walk briskly lower their output of the type of estrogen that causes breast cancer. Fast walking, like aerobic exercise, also improves your memory, enhances your imagination, and decreases your blood sugar, researchers say.

Although the walking habit can't necessarily make you young again, it does slow down the aging process. You have fewer illnesses and more energy. Walking could conceivably hold you at middle age for life.

Almost anyone of any age can start a walking regime. Of course, if you have questions about your health—especially about your heart, lungs, or back, or if you have diabetes or arthritis—you should see a doctor before you start taking long, fast walks.

Finally, a Little Advice

Even if you're not doing strenuous walking, remember to warm up and cool down. Do some body twists and stretches first. A lot of walkers can't touch their toes because walking causes the muscles in the backs of their legs to contract. Unless you gently stretch these muscles and ligaments, they become permanently shortened. Start and end your walk with slow, loose steps. Cool down with some stretches.

Your shoes should have good arch support, a padded lining, breathable uppers, and cushiony soles. One pound on your foot is equivalent to at least five on your back, so don't burden yourself with more shoe than you need. Heavy boots are excessive for the rail-trail hikes.

Remember your hat. It's your defense against hypothermia and your protection against the sun. Your daypack should also include water, lunch, sunblock, insect repellent, a map, a whistle, identification, paper money, and your credit card. I like to be prepared for weather changes with a light waterproof jacket or poncho. Some people carry a walking stick; I don't usually bother, but it may help your balance on hilly sections, and it's good for striking down cobwebs before you walk into them.

Enjoy. Feel the rhythm of a good walk deep in your muscles, feel the breeze against your face, smell the scent of moist green things, and watch the changing scenes. This is your time to connect body and soul.

Logistics

In all but three of these hikes you travel totally under your own foot power from one lodge to the next. You drive your vehicle to the first bed-and-breakfast on your itinerary and there it will stay until you are shuttled back at the end of your trip, unless you arrange with the innkeeper to help you shuttle it to your next destination the morning before your hike. Some innkeepers will do this, others won't. Read the lodging description to determine whether this is a possibility. If you decide to shuttle back to your vehicle at the end of your hike, you can be transported by the last innkeeper or an independent shuttle service. Your shuttle possibilities will be listed in the Key at-a-Glance Information for each hike.

Advance reservations should be made for both shuttles and lodging. Most inns do not provide a packed lunch, and for those who do, the request should be made a few days ahead.

Key at-a-Glance Information

Each trail in this book begins with key information that includes trail length, difficulty, and conditions, as well as scenery, lodging, and shuttle information. The following will help you to understand the information provided.

Length: Distance in miles from one lodge to the next

Difficulty: This provides a description of the degree of physical exertion required.

Elevation change: The figure provided is the gain and/or loss over the course of the hike. In many hikes you both gain and lose this elevation. In areas where the elevation variation is not extreme, the route is simply described as flat or rolling.

Scenery: This describes the predominant characteristics, whether wooded or meadow.

Exposure: This is an indication of the percentage of shade or full sun on the path when the trees are in leaf.

Solitude: Some trails offer perfect solitude—little likelihood of meeting other trail users; others are extremely busy, especially on weekends.

Surface: Trail surfaces may be paved, dirt, or gravel, single track or double.

Trail markings: This indicates whether the trail is blazed throughout or only at road crossings, and how obvious the trail is.

Author's hiking time: This indicates the amount of time it takes a moderately athletic, middle-aged woman to hike the trail. It doesn't factor in sightseeing detours.

Season: Some trails are unsafe during hunting season; others are difficult to track under snowy conditions. This category advises you which seasons to avoid.

Access: A few trails are open only to overnight guests of an inn or resort; most are free and open to the public.

Maps: The maps in this book will help you stay on course, but detailed maps will satisfy your curiosity about the surrounding territory. You may want to avail yourself of the 7.5-minute series U.S. Geological Survey topographic maps or the specific maps mentioned for each hike.

Other uses for trail: Many of these trails are also suitable for mountain biking, cross-country skiing, and horseback riding.

Facilities: This lets you know whether you will be able to purchase snacks or use bathroom facilities along this trail.

Shuttle: This category lets you know which lodging establishments will provide a shuttle back to your car and whether independent shuttle services are available.

Lodging info: The recommended lodging the author has visited is listed here.

Alternative lodging: Other sources of lodging are named here. Some may be listed as alternatives because they require a two-night minimum, offer no food facilities, or pose other inconveniences for hikers.

Key to pricing scale for lodging:

$—$25–55

$$—$56–75

$$$—$76–95

$$$$—$96–120

$$$$$—$121–150

$$$$$$—$151+

Rates are per room, double or single occupancy, with breakfast unless otherwise noted. A few inns require a two-night minimum stay on holiday weekends. Call first to determine if you will be affected.

Getting there: This category gives directions from the major roads traversing the area.

West Virginia Hikes

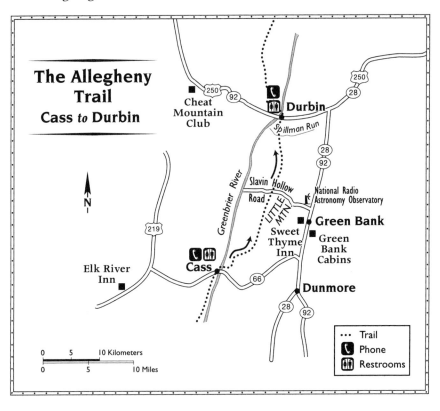

The Allegheny
Trail
Cass *to* Durbin

Getting there:

To reach Elk River Inn at Slatyfork, take Route 39 west from the Virginia border or US 219 north from Lewisburg to Marlinton. From Marlinton, take US 219 north about 15 miles. Elk River Inn is on your left before the general store.

To get to Cheat Mountain Club, take Interstate 81 to US 250 west and continue on 250 for 65 miles. Take Route 28 south to the junction of US 250/Route 92 and go west for 12.5 miles to the club entrance road.

The Allegheny Trail

Cass to Durbin

This section of the 330-mile Allegheny Trail begins beside the tracks of Cass Scenic Railroad State Park's working steam train and runs through rhododendron thickets in West Virginia's unbroken wilderness, past views of the world's largest radio telescope.

The Lowdown

Plenty of great inns exist in the Mountain State, but because none are located within easy walking distance of this splendid wilderness trail, we persuaded the managers of the Elk River Inn and the Cheat Mountain Club to shuttle guests from points where the trail passes telephone booths in nearby towns. You will start this hike at the bridge in front of Cass Scenic Railroad State Park, after a morning shuttle from Elk River Inn.

This is a strenuous hike over mountains that just don't quit. The nearly-18-mile trek between Cass and Durbin can be done in a day by relative tenderfeet (ours), but you'll probably enjoy it much, much more if you break it into two less energetic days. A short detour into the town of Green Bank, with its cabins and vegan bed-and-breakfast, adds almost 5 miles to the trip—for a grand total of nearly 23 miles.

You will spot the yellow blazes of the Allegheny Trail as it passes over the Greenbrier River bridge in front of the train station and takes an immediate turn left onto a dirt road. In about one and a half miles, the road veers away from the Greenbrier and goes uphill past a large house surrounded by retired Volvos, Peugeots, and dogs. The sign on the gate says "private property," but don't let that deter you. Follow the yellow blazes along an old railroad grade through lush fern gardens and hemlock thickets. Soon you're on Monongahela National Forest land.

Key at-a-Glance Information

Length: Cass to Green Bank: 10 miles; Green Bank to Durbin: 12.7 miles (Cass to Durbin without Green Bank detour: 17.7 miles)

Difficulty: Fairly strenuous

Elevation gain and loss: 1,040 feet

Scenery: Mostly wooded with views of Deer Creek Valley

Exposure: Shady–95   Moderate–5

Solitude: Perfect

Surface: Single-track dirt path, overgrown in places

Trail markings: Yellow blaze, not well marked at road crossings

Author's hiking time: Cass to Green Bank: 6 hours; Green Bank to Durbin: 7.5 hours

Season: Avoid the November hunting session; trail is difficult to follow when snowy.

Access: No permits or fees

Maps: *Hiking Guide to the Allegheny Trail* can be ordered for $8 by writing to WVSTA, P.O. Box 4042, Charleston, WV 25364.

Other uses for trail: Horseback riding

Facilities: No bathrooms or stores on this section of the Allegheny Trail, except the Cass General Store and Durbin restaurants. Greenbank has a BP station with food and bathrooms.

Shuttle: Manager of Cheat Mountain Club can shuttle guests who have made prior arrangements. Otherwise, make reservations for a prepaid shuttle with Elk River Inn and Touring Center at (304) 572-3771.

Lodging info:

Elk River Inn and Touring Center, Slatyfork, West Virginia (304) 572-3771; www.ertc.com; $–$$$

Sweet Thyme Inn, Route 92/28, Green Bank, West Virginia (304) 456-5535; www.sweetthymeinn.com; $$–$$$$ (meals extra)

Cheat Mountain Club, Shavers Fork Road, Durbin, West Virginia (304) 456-4627; www.cheatmountainclub.com; $$–$$$$$

Alternative lodging:

Cass Scenic Railroad State Park (call (800) CALLWVA) rents six- to ten-person, fully equipped, former-logging-employee houses. Two-day rental is required on weekends. In Green Bank, you may opt to stay a night at the rustic Green Bank Cottage and Green Bank Log Cabins (call (304) 456-3470 or (304) 456-4410). You will need to get your victuals at the BP gas station or make dinner reservations at the Sweet Thyme Inn.

We hoped to see bears on our trip—downwind and from a distance, of course—but we never did. We did, however, see evidence of their presence. The bears in this area are not subtle about letting you know they're about. You'll see signs of them in raked blueberry bushes, in berry-filled scat along the stream, and on occasional paw-shredded trees. Eastern black bears haven't had a reputation for being aggressive since the days of Daniel Boone, but a mother with cubs could make an exception. As you hike, make noise to let them know you're passing through their territory, and if you do spot one, back up and give it plenty of space. Don't climb a tree—they're better at this than you are. Black bears are fast runners too, though they can be a bit clumsy going downhill. After a hiker makes the 900-foot climb from Cass, I'd put my racing money on the bear.

Half a mile after crossing into national forest land, you'll ford a small creek and follow it through rugged country for another half mile uphill, passing through tree trunks scarred and blackened by an old fire. As you gain the top, you earn a good overlook of eastern Deer Creek Valley. For the next two and a half miles, the trail winds along the crest of Little Mountain (elevation 3,350 feet) on an old logging road.

In the early spring especially, you'll get surreal views of the giant metal chrysanthemums at the National Radio Astronomy Observatory (NRAO) at Green Bank. The main telescope is 485 feet tall and can accommodate almost two football fields side by side in its collecting dish. In fact, it is the world's largest fully steerable radio telescope.

The old logging road you're traveling eventually joins the former Little Mountain Trail (which is blue-blazed) on this ledge and passes into land owned by the national observatory. A cell phone is no link to the outside world here; no relay towers are allowed to interfere with the NRAO's signals.

Just over seven and one quarter miles from Cass, start down a small incline through widely spaced oak trees and turn abruptly right onto the Slavin Hollow/Hosterman Road. To break up your trip into two days, detour down the unused, dirt-track Slavin Hollow Road about two and a half miles through forest and the observatory park fields to the village of Green Bank.

Slavin Hollow Road will take you to the NRAO tour center and gift shop. The town and Sweet Thyme Inn are another mile right on Route 92. Walk on the left shoulder watching for fast-moving vehicles.

The NRAO offers guided tours of their facilities from 9 A.M. to 4 P.M. daily, from Memorial Day through Labor Day and on weekends in the fall. The observatory has a replica of the 1930s-era Jansky Antenna—the first to intercept radio waves from outside of the solar system—and the telescope that Grote Reber built in his backyard to track cosmic radio

The author looks for the next yellow blaze on the Allegheny Trail.

waves in the early 1940s. You will see at least seven major telescopes on your tour. On Wednesday nights, the NRAO hosts special "behind the scenes" tours that give participants the chance to make their own astronomical images or view the planets in detail. (Call (304) 456-2150 for information.)

Your dining choices in town are the vegan Sweet Thyme Inn (advance reservations required) or sandwiches from the BP gas station.

Day Two

After a healthful breakfast, leave the Sweet Thyme Inn and retrace your steps up Route 92 and Slavin Hollow Road to the trail. As you leave the Slavin Hollow, the trail climbs to the top of the mountain and begins to descend through low trees. The path becomes so overgrown with heath brush you could have trouble seeing your feet. Edward Pride, the volunteer who oversees the trail in this area, estimates about four or five hikers a month travel this section in summer, not enough to tramp down the new growth. You may need to rely on the yellow blazes more than the path here.

Laurel Run, at the bottom of a slope, looks like a prime bear refuge with its dark thickets and minnowed waters. This is an open area with remnants of old beaver ponds. The trail soon heads back up Little Mountain, gaining 600 feet; some stretches are steep. When you reach the crest, it's an easy, almost flat stroll along a grassy path for the next three miles or so. You brush against hay-scented ferns that actually smell like potpourri. This mingles with the curry fragrance emitted by witch hazel nuts crunching under your feet.

The blue-blazed Little Mountain Trail goes off to the left and the loosely marked Allegheny Trail slips downhill under dark evergreens to Brush Run. This stream is often so high you may want to take your shoes off or search for a more shallow crossing 20 yards downstream.

The trail ascends again in two short, steep sections and then traverses Sandy Ridge. The Allegheny descends to cross Spillman Run near a beaver dam and then descends again to the Greenbrier River near a log yard. Cross the Greenbrier on the River Road to US 250 and turn left into Durbin. There is a restaurant here, an ice creamery, and the Durbin and Greenbrier excursion railroad, but what you probably want most is phone contact with your shuttle from Cheat Mountain Club.

Your reward at the end of an invigorating trip is Cheat Mountain, a place of red spruce and ferny hummocks that seems 1,500 miles farther north than it really is. The Club's spruce-timbered lodge always seems to have a fire roaring in the fireplace for those who've earned the right to snooze in front of the hearth like old dogs.

Elk River Inn and Touring Center
Slatyfork, West Virginia

Gil and Mary Willis' 100-year old homestead on the banks of Elk River provides a nice setting for fishing and mountain biking outings. Don't know much about fly-fishing? Guided expeditions and instruction are available. And of course the folks at Elk River are happy to shuttle you from Cass, Durbin, or Green Bank for a fee.

You have several options for lodging at Elk River. The Elk River Inn contains five upstairs bedrooms, each with its own bath. Rooms are decorated with country antiques and sleep two to four people. A downstairs sitting area with a TV and a phone is available for guests' use. The bar, restaurant, and a small outdoor-supply shop are also located in this building.

The Elk River Farmhouse, across the parking lot, is an economical option with five rooms, three shared baths, a cozy common area, and a communal hot tub on the porch. Elk River also offers lodging in two-bedroom cabins. Breakfast is not included in the price of the cabins.

The Restaurant at Elk River offers specialties including linguini in pesto cream, salmon with tamari glaze, and blackened ribeye with tomatillo salsa. The whole-wheat French bread is good and allows you to feel a little righteous when you're enjoying it. Desserts such as chocolate pecan pie and cheesecake with raspberry sauce are usually available. West Virginia Brewing Company's microbrews are on tap and so is local old-time music on some weekends.

On Thursdays, the restaurant offers an international buffet featuring a different nationality each week. It is closed Mondays through Wednesdays.

Sweet Thyme Inn
Green Bank, West Virginia

The National Radio Astronomy Observatory chose to locate in Green Bank because the sky is clear and uncluttered with civilization's towers and signals. The Sweet Thyme Inn chose Green Bank because the air is clean and healthful. Pat and Chuck Merithew sold the inn they operated in Vermont near the Appalachian Trail to open Sweet Thyme Inn in September 1999. They have remodeled the 1890 homestead into four large guest rooms with private baths. They have also created a small trail behind the home. Healthfulness and environmental sensitivity are the missions of this inn, which uses sheets and towels woven from chemical-free, unbleached cotton and serves organic vegan food (no meat, eggs, or dairy products).

Even if you aren't a vegetarian, Pat and Chuck Merithew's concoctions such as herb-walnut ravioli and mushroom roll-ups will tempt you.

Two hearty meals are prepared from scratch; the desserts are sweetened with unrefined natural ingredients. Freshly ground organic coffees and a variety of organic teas are available. Meals are an extra $25, and you should make dinner reservations when you reserve your room.

Green Bank Cottage and Green Bank Log Cabins
Green Bank, West Virginia

Furnished, rustic 1800 log cabins built of hand-hewn logs are located near the Sweet Thyme Inn on Route 92. These have bathrooms. A more rustic cabin (with an outhouse) and a two-bedroom former schoolhouse are located a half mile from the NRAO visitor's center. Extremely reasonable rates.

Cheat Mountain Club
Durbin, West Virginia

Cheat Mountain Club sits beside Shavers Fork, high in a land apart from the rest of West Virginia. The ferns and moss grow thick under the spruce, and the peaty earth springs under your footstep. All around you is the scent of moist, evergreen forest. You're in the territory of bears and wildcats—perhaps even mountain lions.

The clubhouse was built in 1887 by the Cheat Mountain Sportsman's Association as a private hunting and fishing preserve. The elite club entertained such notables as John Burroughs, Henry Ford, and Thomas Edison. In the 1930s, it was used as a hunting retreat by railroad and logging companies. Not until 1987 did Cheat Mountain Club open its ten rooms to the general public.

Since then, nature lovers have been coming to the historic lodge for hiking, mountain biking, fishing, canoeing, or retreating in general.

Birdwatchers are especially fond of seeing rose-breasted grosbeaks, winter wrens, and a variety of warblers seldom sighted in southern locations.

This is a true getaway, with no room phones, televisions, fax machines, or road traffic except for lodge visitors. As the hip waders and fishing rods hung on the porch imply, fly-fishing is the main attraction at CMC.

All rooms except the private Spruce Suite share country-club style baths for men and women on the second floor. Each room is furnished with a lavatory and a CMC bathrobe. A third-floor dormitory style room contains one king bed and four twins and shares the downstairs bathroom facilities. Three daily meals are included in the lodging rate.

The Allegheny Trail

Huntersville to Cass

The Allegheny Trail winds along 330 miles of backbone ridges, hollows, and high bogs, through some of West Virginia's wildest, prettiest territory. In this section, the trail passes over several mountain forests and along the Greenbrier River to a restored logging village with its own working steam train.

The Lowdown

The Carriage House Inn in Huntersville is your starting point for this section of the Allegheny Trail. With a little prior notice, innkeeper Jeannie Dunham will drop hikers off where the yellow-blazed trail turns left off Route 28 onto Thorny Creek Road, across from the Buckskin Boy Scout Reservation.

The Allegheny Trail actually crosses Route 39 somewhere (we couldn't locate it in a half-hour search) about a mile from the Carriage House, but starting there would make for an extremely strenuous 25-mile trek. Not much of a decision here. We set off across from the scout camp on the dirt-surfaced Thorny Creek Road, striking off on an old logging road to the right after one-tenth of a mile.

The signs of wildlife are immediate. Within a half mile, we stumbled upon the skeleton of a four-foot snake coiled in our path, the scat of a large animal that had obviously eaten a mammal for breakfast, and a blueberry patch where the soil appeared raked by giant paws.

Despite indications of wildlife, the forest remained exceptionally quiet in summer. We had the sensation of being the strangers in neon running gear who had bumbled into a country store and brought conversation to a halt. Everything seemed to have ceased breathing while the forest waited for us to pass.

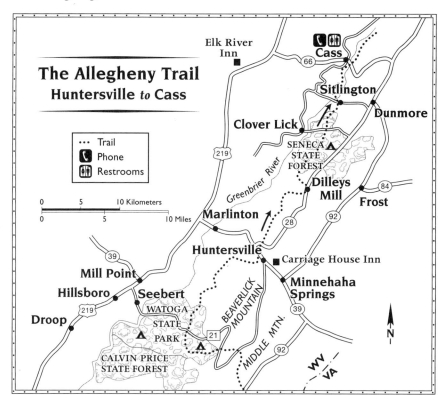

Getting there:

To reach the Carriage House Inn at Huntersville, take Interstate 64 to the White Sulphur Springs exit, then head north on Route 92 until it hits Route 39 near Minnehaha Springs; then turn left (west) on 39 and go to Huntersville, where the Carriage House is on your right. To get to Cass, take Route 28/92 north from Route 39 at Minnehaha Springs, then go left for three miles on Route 66.

Key at-a-Glance Information

Length: Boy Scout Camp to Cass: 15.1 miles

Difficulty: Moderately strenuous

Elevation gain and loss: 880 feet

Scenery: Mostly wooded with views of Greenbrier River and countryside

Exposure: Shady–85 Moderate–5 Exposed–10

Solitude: Perfect

Surface: Single-track dirt path

Trail markings: Yellow blaze, not well marked at road crossings

Author's hiking time: Boy Scout Camp to Cass: 8 hours

Season: Avoid the November hunting season; the trail is difficult to follow when snow is on the ground.

Access: No permits or fees

Maps: *Hiking Guide to the Allegheny Trail* can be ordered for $8 by writing to: WVSTA, P.O. Box 4042, Charleston, WV 25364.

Other uses for trail: Horseback riding

Facilities: No bathrooms or stores on this section of the Allegheny Trail, except at the Cass General Store

Shuttle: Owners of Carriage House Inn and Elk River Inn and Touring Center will shuttle guests for a fee. Make prior arrangements.

Lodging info:

Carriage House Inn, Route 39, Huntersville, West Virginia
(304) 799-6706; $$–$$$

Elk River Inn and Touring Center, Slatyfork, West Virginia
(304) 572-3771; www.ertc.com; $–$$$

Alternative lodging:

Seneca State Park Cabins (call (800) CALL WVA) rents rustic cabins (gas lights, pit toilets) Monday through Thursday. On weekends the furnished cabins must be rented for two nights, and in the summer they must be rented for a week. Cass Scenic Railroad State Park (call (800) CALL WVA) rents six- to ten-person, fully equipped, former logging-company homes. A two-night minimum stay is required on weekends.

We didn't see any bears, but Mike Maxwell of Charleston, our hiking companion farther up the trail, had encountered one falling out of a tree only a few days before. "It squalled when it fell," he said. "Now that can put goosebumps on you. Luckily, it looked at me and ran the other way."

The logging road dwindles to a single track after a half mile and then to an indistinct passage signaled only by gold blazes on the oaks and hickories as it ascends Thorny Creek Mountain. It passes through laurel thickets and an oak grove with spaces large enough for a tight game of softball. Hikers are sparse on this section of the Allegheny Trail; Vicky Shears, section coordinator, says she has worked on the trail whole summer weekends without seeing another hiker. The Allegheny Trail does not receive federal or state funding and has relied upon volunteers like Shears since its beginning in 1975.

Thorny Creek Mountain is surprisingly remote. After a mile and a half, the trail joins a dirt track called Kronmiller Road for 200 yards—a road that seems to see its only traffic during hunting season. Cell phones don't work out here because there are no relay towers.

We walked hard all morning, hard enough to hear our pulses thudding in our throats, and when we sat down at one of Seneca State Park's log shelters for lunch, we realized we had gone less than five miles and had to go more than ten more before we would eat again. Allegheny Trail miles seem at least twice as long as road miles.

The trail through the park briefly joins the River Cabin Road toward Seneca Lake. This is not a swimming lake, but you can find such amenities as bathrooms, rustic cabins, a kiosk dispensing maps of the Allegheny Trail, a ranger station, and a fire tower. The lake is stocked with trout in the spring and fall. After one-tenth of a mile, the Allegheny turns off onto a grassy roadway into the woods and descends the mountain along a small stream, crossing over Laurel Run after a half mile.

This trail never spares its users an aerobic workout; in fact, it seems to go out of its way to provide strenuous climbs. As it ascends to what surely seems the summits of Little, Thomas, and Thorny Creek Mountains, the crests flatten out and reveal new heights. After six or seven hours on the trail, you cease thinking and just step, step, step methodically.

The scrubby, wind-beaten vegetation on mountaintops mirrors the hikers' stoicism. Like the autumn woods getting ready to go dormant until spring, we wanted to lie very still for a long, long time after we'd made several ascents.

As the trail enters Seneca State Forest for the climb up 3,200-foot Thomas Mountain, you see increasing evidence of natural mayhem. Downed trees lie along the path near the summit, many clutching a small vegetable garden's worth of earth in their roots. Others are fractured at the trunk from a violent twist. Flee this place in a storm.

Steam engines make daily runs at Cass Railroad State Park all summer and on fall weekends.

The hike gets easier after you pass the crest of Thomas Mountain. In a half mile you hit County Road 12 and turn left. Follow this narrow dirt road for a mile to the banks of the Greenbrier River and the hamlet of Sitlington. After crossing the river on a metal bridge, turn right to join the Greenbrier Trail for a relatively flat walk of just under three and a half miles to Cass. You can summon your shuttle from a phone outside the general store.

You may want to spend a rest day at Cass Scenic Railroad State Park, where former logging-camp houses can be rented (again, on weekends they must be rented for two nights), and the restaurant food is ample and country style. The idea of letting the steam energy of an old Shay locomotive pull you to the top of Cheat Mountain may sound very appealing at this point.

Carriage House Inn
Huntersville, West Virginia

Carriage House Inn owner Jeannie Dunham lived in southern California for at least a decade before returning to her family's West Virginia roots. Her sumptuous meals reflect the best of both worlds. Breakfast, for instance,

can be homemade Pocahontas County pear butter and exotically spiced whole-wheat French toast with a salad of mixed fresh fruit. Or peach pancakes with homemade raspberry sauce. She will also make dinners and boxed lunches if you give her a little notice.

All six guest rooms in the 1852 Carriage House have private baths and cable television. You sleep in canopy beds under handmade quilts and can fill your water bottles with full-bodied water from an artesian well.

The comfortable guest living room has a television and a telephone. And you can do your gift shopping in Dunham's large store without even leaving the grounds. The shop features the work of local artists, as well as a variety of gift items and antiques. One room is dedicated to teddy bears and the loft features the work of longtime local artist Betty Jo Kramer-Vydra.

Elk River Inn and Touring Center
Slatyfork, West Virginia

Gil and Mary Willis' 100-year-old homestead on the banks of the Elk River provides a nice setting to hang out for a day of fly-fishing or mountain biking. Don't know much about fly-fishing? Guided expeditions and instruction are available. The folks at Elk River Inn and Touring Center in Slatyfork can shuttle you from Cass or Sitlington for a fee.

You have several options in lodging at Elk River. The Elk River Inn contains five upstairs bedrooms, each with its own bath. Rooms are decorated with country antiques and sleep two to four people.

The Elk River Farmhouse, across the parking lot, is an economical option with five rooms, three shared baths, a cozy common area, and a communal hot tub on the porch. Elk River also offers lodging in two-bedroom cabins, which does not include breakfast in the price.

The Restaurant at Elk River offers specialties including linguini in pesto cream, salmon with tamari glaze, and blackened ribeye with tomatillo salsa. Desserts such as chocolate pecan pie or cheesecake with raspberry sauce are just desserts for hikers who've climbed three mountains. West Virginia Brewing Company's microbrews are on tap, and an assortment of imported beers and wines are available by the bottle or the glass. On Thursdays, the restaurant offers an international buffet; it is closed Mondays through Wednesdays.

Canaan Valley State Park to Blackwater Falls State Park

Passing over 3,800-foot Canaan Mountain, this trail connects two state park lodges. Along the way, hikers encounter spruce forest and high bogs—terrain that looks more like Canada than West Virginia.

The Lowdown

> *"To Canaan's land I'm on my way,*
> *Where the soul never dies.*
> *Where all is joy, peace, and love*
> *And the soul of man never dies."*
>
> —hymn written by William Golden

You can get a feeling for eternity sitting out behind Canaan Valley Resort's lodge, watching the light fade over miles of high marsh and forest. Out here it seems a lot more stays the same than changes. Life seems to go on forever in some form. Could there be any small, petty thinking in Canaan Valley?

I hear a distant "Who, who for you?" A barn owl? A little later, a woodcock circles with a high "chee." A doe saunters toward the lodge, stopping to rub the top of her head with back hoof. No fear here.

Canaan Valley (pronounced cuh-nane by locals) is a place of quiet beauty, where the summers are mild and the winter snows deep (snowfall averages 175 inches annually). Frosts have been recorded every month of the year, and cool air slides down the mountains at night, leaving a dreamy fog over the valley almost every morning between May and November.

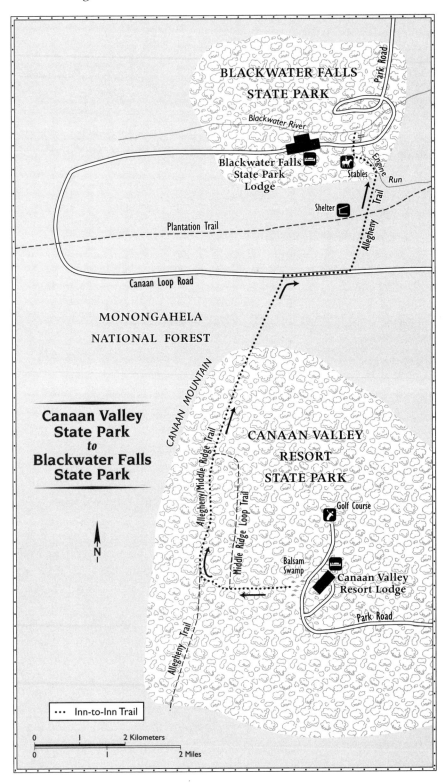

BLACKWATER FALLS
STATE PARK

Blackwater River

Park Road

Engine Run Trail

Blackwater Falls
State Park
Lodge

Stables

Run

Shelter

Allegheny Trail

Plantation Trail

Canaan Loop Road

MONONGAHELA

NATIONAL FOREST

CANAAN MOUNTAIN

**Canaan Valley
State Park
to
Blackwater Falls
State Park**

N

CANAAN VALLEY

RESORT

STATE PARK

Golf Course

Allegheny/Middle Ridge Trail

Middle Ridge Loop Trail

Balsam
Swamp

Canaan Valley
Resort Lodge

Park Road

Allegheny Trail

··· Inn-to-Inn Trail

0   1   2 Kilometers

0   1   2 Miles

Key at-a-Glance Information

Length: 8 miles

Difficulty: Moderate, with a sustained climb in the middle

Elevation gain: About 700 feet

Scenery: Pleasant, with occasional views of the valley

Exposure: Shady–80   Moderate–10   Exposed–10

Solitude: Near perfect; an occasional cyclist

Surface: Dirt path; forest road for 1.2 miles

Trail markings: Yellow blazes

Author's hiking time: 4 hours

Season: Year-round; it is used as a cross-country ski trail in winter.

Access: No permits or fees

Maps: *Canaan Valley Resort Map and Trail Guide* available at Canaan Valley Lodge desk and Blackwater Falls State Park trail map available at Blackwater Falls Lodge desk

Other uses for trail: Mountain biking, cross-country skiing

Facilities: No bathrooms or civilization on this trail

Shuttle: Highland Scene Tours, which also rents bikes and leads interpretive hikes; call (304) 259-5880.

Lodging info:

Canaan Valley Resort at Canaan Valley State Park
Canaan Valley Road, Davis, West Virginia
(304) 866-4121 or (800) 622-4121; www.canaanresort.com; $$–$$$

Blackwater Lodge at Blackwater Falls State Park, Davis, West Virginia
(304) 259-5216 or (800) CALL WVA; www.blackwaterfalls.com; $–$$$

Getting there:

Located in the Potomac Highlands region of West Virginia, Canaan Valley and Blackwater Falls are accessible from the south by taking US 33 to Harman, then Route 32 north. The parks stand about nine miles apart by road. From the north, take US 219 to Thomas, then Route 32 south to the parks.

Hikers must jump between stepping stones in
the bogs atop Canaan Mountain.

Underneath its apparent tranquillity, Canaan Valley is still in recovery mode. In the earlier part of the century, this country was logged out of its spruce and hemlock forests. Fires kindled by logging detritus swept over the land, burning the deep, peaty soil that had taken thousands of years to develop.

The vegetation we see today has somehow managed to migrate back into this cool, humid climate and mix with species introduced by man. Many of these plants—including red spruce, balsam fir, highbush cranberry, swamp saxifrage, and Jacob's ladder—are considered boreal species, two vegetation zones below tundra. Portions of the Canaan Valley have been designated a National Natural Landmark because of the unusual Canadian forest plant life and the 6,700 acres of fragile upcountry wetlands.

The sheltering Canaan and Cabin Mountains create a wind shadow over the valley. Strong winds carrying snow or rain over the tops of these mountains dump their precipitation in areas of weak, irregular air movement, making Canaan greener or whiter than surrounding areas. Most of West Virginia lies in a cloud belt, causing twice as many overcast days as sunny ones. Adjust your expectations and wardrobe for the cool, rainy weather that gives Canaan Valley its beauty.

To begin the trek between the two parks, walk down the slope behind the Canaan Valley lodge and along the paved Golf Course Road one-tenth of a mile right to the Balsam Swamp Overlook, where you will turn right on the Middle Ridge Loop Trail. You will see a small signpost almost as soon as you spot the path. Continue along this trail, past an incoming trail on your right (the return loop for the Middle Ridge Loop Trail).

This narrow footpath climbs uphill, and after a half mile, it merges with the yellow-blazed Allegheny Trail. The hay-scented ferns grow as thick as wheat here, and you can hear wood thrush calls cascading through red maples, yellow birch, and hobblebush. Small creatures seem to be ransacking the underbrush, always out of your line of sight no matter how quickly you turn.

Turn right, following the merged Allegheny/Middle Ridge along and over a ridge through running pine and other club mosses. You descend to open meadows and a marsh—good bird watching territory. Down here the deer are wild enough to bound away at your approach; they don't stick around looking for a handout, admiration, or whatever keeps them posing like Disney World creatures at the lodge.

Laurel and rhododendron thickets at the edge of the swamp are thick, but not as thick as when Canaan was discovered by Lord Fairfax's surveyors in 1746. The first white men did not see the valley as a land of milk and honey. Writes surveyor Thomas Lewis of the expedition: "The river we called Styx for the dismal appearance of the place being sufficient to strike terror into any human creature. Ye laurels and spruce grow so thick that one cannot have the least prospect of seeing except they look upwards."

After skirting the marshy area for about seven-tenths of a mile, the trail heads up Canaan Mountain. Signs caution of a steep ascent, but this warning probably is directed at skiers or bikers; for hikers, the incline is not exceptionally taxing. During the climb, the trail crosses from Canaan Valley State Park to Monongahela National Forest.

Water seeps out of the ground at the summit in little bogs covered with sphagnum mosses, arrowroot, and dwarf cherry shrubs. Bluets and pink lady's slippers also tolerate the acid soil. The club mosses here look like miniature pines and cedars. Ground pine has been used by campers to stuff mattresses, but the plant is too slow growing to survive much collecting and is protected in many states. The trail is so boggy here you'll have to hop between rocks and logs to keep your feet dry.

The spruce-covered mountaintop (elevation 3,800 feet) is quieter than the valley. Occasionally, a junco emits a snapping sound like rocks being whacked together underwater. You turn right on the dirt Canaan Loop Road and follow it just under one and a quarter miles, past high bogs and dense spruce forest, before turning left down the mountain. The path glows from a bed of white quartz pebbles. The scent of ferns and flowers mixes in shafts of sun, lifting up a strawberry scent. You descend from spruce and hemlock into hardwoods—maple and beech.

After a mile, you pass the Plantation Trail that leads to Canaan Mountain Shelter. The trail follows and crosses Engine Run, whose golden water ripples over white pebbles past dark roots and black rocks. The Blackwater Falls naturalist says the amber color is the result of decaying hemlock and spruce needles. The dark water is produced when tannic acids leach from these fallen leaves. If the bed of the creek were slate-gray, the water could seem as dark as Bombay tea.

At the bottom of the mountain, the trail crosses Engine Run on a Blackwater Falls State Park bridge and becomes a broad, well-groomed path to the stables. From the stables, turn left on the paved park road to the Blackwater Lodge.

Canaan Valley Resort
Canaan Valley State Park

If you leave your ground-floor room door open too long at Canaan Valley Resort, you're likely to get a hoofed visitor. The deer are that friendly at this 6,000-acre state park. With the forest and wetland literally at your back door, you're bound to see and hear a few of the 280 species of mammals, birds, reptiles, and amphibians that live here.

The park features an especially active schedule of nature programs to explain its diverse wildlife resources; you can choose among birding walks, butterfly watches, fishing expeditions, lectures, and more.

Three motel-like lodge buildings offer 250 guest rooms, complete with satellite TV, in-room movies, phones, heat and air conditioning, and complimentary coffee. Efficiency rooms and fully equipped cottages for two to eight people are also available. The resort offers golf, indoor and outdoor swimming pools, a hot tub, saunas, tennis, and skiing and skating in season.

The lodge dining room serves breakfast, lunch, and dinner buffets, as well as tasty entrees, and it offers an awe-inspiring view from the two-story windows. With prior notice, staff members will prepare a sandwich lunch for your hike. Snacks are sold in the gift shop.

In the budget season of March through May, room rates are 30 percent lower.

Blackwater Lodge
Blackwater Falls State Park

Blackwater Lodge sits on the south rim of Blackwater River canyon, providing its overnight and dining guests with a sweeping view of the densely forested gorge. Although numerous observation points offer panoramic views of the five-story falls, the stone overlook in front of the lodge gives one of best.

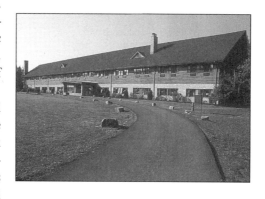

The rambling log and stone lodge exudes the ambiance of a grand old park in the tradition of Yellowstone. Even the upstairs rooms smell of smoke and pine. Each of the 54 guest rooms is air conditioned, although that's not really necessary here—summer-night temperatures may dip into the 40s. All rooms have private baths, phones, and television.

The lodge also features a game room, an indoor pool, and a sitting room with a cavernous fireplace. A large, wood-paneled restaurant overlooking the canyon serves regional specialties. A gift shop offers a nice selection of West Virginia glass, books, handcrafted items, and other souvenirs.

Because Blackwater Falls is a four-season destination, nature and recreation programs go on all year. Guests may participate in craft workshops, slide shows, nature lectures, and guided hikes.

Room rates are 20 to 25 percent lower in November, March, and April.

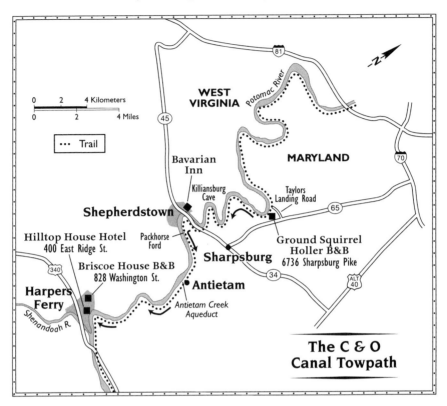

The C & O
Canal Towpath

Getting there:

Ground Squirrel Holler is located eight miles southeast of Interstate 70 from the Sharpsburg/Hagerstown exit on Route 65.

The Bavarian Inn is on Route 480 on the West Virginia side of the Rumsey Bridge.

To get to the Briscoe and Hilltop Houses, take US 340 to Harpers Ferry. If you're coming from the west, you'll see a sign for Bolivar/Harpers Ferry and a stop light. Turn left there, and take Washington Street toward downtown. If you're coming from the east, cross the first two bridges in town, take a right onto Union Street and another right onto Washington. Briscoe House will be on your left. To get to Hilltop House, continue on Washington to the top of the hill, then turn left on Jackson Street and right on Ridge Street. Hilltop House is the last house on the left.

The C&O Canal Towpath

Taylors Landing, Maryland to Harpers Ferry, West Virginia

This flat, easy walk along the Potomac River takes you through the remnants of a bygone industrial era between historic Civil War towns.

The Lowdown

For a century, the C&O Canal was the commercial lifeblood of communities along the Potomac River. The idea to create a viable commercial waterway along the Potomac began with George Washington, but the project was not started in earnest until 1828, when workers, mostly immigrants, began digging the canal with picks and shovels. Due to financial problems, floods, worker disputes, and epidemics that decimated the workforce, it took 22 years to build the canal. When completed in 1850, the project included 11 stone aqueducts carrying the canal over larger streams and more than 200 culverts funneling small streams under the canal.

The C&O's 74 locks raised boats from tidewater level in Georgetown to 605 feet above sea level in Cumberland, Maryland. The canal bed was usually 6 feet deep, and it was 60 feet wide at its top, slanting down to 40 feet wide at its base. A trip up the river took four to six days in an empty canal boat and six to eight when the boat was loaded. Mules walked along the towpath pulling the boat; often another team rested on board. Children would start training to drive mules as young as five or six years old.

The canal's vitality was short lived, as floods and increasing competition from the railroads took its toll. The canal closed for good in 1924. Today the C&O Canal National Historical Park preserves pieces of America's transportation history, and thousands of people visit it each

Key at-a-Glance Information

Length: Taylors Landing to Shepherdstown: 10 miles; Shepherdstown to Harpers Ferry: 12.5 miles

Difficulty: Flat and easy

Elevation gain: Negligible

Scenery: Mostly woods, with occasional views of river and canal ruins

Exposure: Shady–70   Moderate–15   Exposed–15

Solitude: Busy on weekends

Surface: Packed dirt double track

Trail markings: Only at crossings, but trail is obvious

Author's hiking time: Taylors Landing to Shepherdstown: 4 hours; Shepherdstown to Harpers Ferry: 5 hours

Season: Year-round

Access: No permits or fees

Maps: Chesapeake and Ohio Canal National Historical Park map and guide, available from the park visitors' centers in Georgetown, Great Falls Tavern, Williamsport, Hancock, Cumberland, and the park headquarters at Box 4, Sharpsburg, Maryland 21782 (call (301) 739-4200)

Other uses for trail: Biking, cross-country skiing; horseback riding from Swain's Lock to the trail's terminus in Cumberland, Maryland

Facilities: Snacks sold on weekends at C&O Canal Trail Store at milepost 76.7; toilets at mileposts 79.7, 75, 67, 65, and 63

Shuttle: Jefferson County Taxi Service (call (304) 725-3794) or C&O Canal Bicycling (call (301) 834-5180); Briscoe House innkeepers will shuttle their own guests who have made prior arrangements.

Lodging info:

Ground Squirrel Holler Bed and Breakfast, 6736 Sharpsburg Pike Sharpsburg, Maryland, (301) 432-8288; $$–$$$

Bavarian Inn, Route 34, Shepherdstown, West Virginia (304) 876-2551; www.bavarianinnwv.com; $$$–$$$$$$ (meals extra)

Briscoe House Bed and Breakfast, 828 Washington Street Harpers Ferry, West Virginia, (304) 535-2416; www.bbonline.com/wv/briscoe; $$–$$$

Hilltop House Hotel, 400 East Ridge Street, Harpers Ferry, West Virginia (304) 535-2132; www.hilltophousehotel.net; $–$$$$$

Alternative lodging:

In Harpers Ferry, the Jefferson County Convention and Visitors Bureau (call (800) 848 TOUR) can give you other listings. In Shepherdstown, you can walk to the Thomas Shepherd Inn (call (304) 876-3715) or Bellevue Bed and Breakfast (call (304) 876-0889).

weekend. The park stretches 184 miles along the Potomac River between Cumberland, Maryland, and the nation's capital, but only in the middle can a walker find lodging spaced at reasonable distances.

After starting the day with a hearty continental breakfast at the Ground Squirrel Holler Bed and Breakfast, you will hike almost one and one-quarter miles along the shoulder of the narrow Taylors Landing Road to the C&O Canal towpath. Head east (left) on the alder- and willow-lined towpath beside the Potomac (which will be on your right). Fragments of the canal will appear on your left.

In the next four miles, you'll pass good horseshoe-bend fishing spots and beds of wild phlox. The trail winds and twists with the river. At milepost 79.4, you reach the site of Lock 40, damaged by Jubal Early's Confederate forces in the Civil War. Sources say his troops also burned about 60 canal boats to make sure supplies of fuel and grain wouldn't reach the U.S. capital.

You may notice that the shores of the Potomac are littered with small shells. These are the shells of native freshwater mussels, snails, and the abundant non-native Asiatic clams. The mussels are desirable because they filter algae and organic debris out of the freshwater, cleaning up the river. Unfortunately, one species is endangered and several others are not doing well because of pollution, silt, and competition from the Asiatic clams.

Snyders Landing at milepost 76.7 is named for the Snyder coal and grain warehouse that washed away in the 1936 flood. On weekends, Barron's C&O Canal Trail Store on the hill above the canal serves snacks. Look for the footbridge leading to the store. In the spring, you can see a proliferation of flowers here, including Solomon's seal, jewelweed, sweet cicely, and cream violet.

This section of the trail is rife with Civil War history. A mile farther east (milepost 75.7) the C&O passes a number of shallow caves, including the Killiansburg Cave where Sharpsburg citizens hid out during the bloody 1862 Battle of Antietam. A half mile upstream is the Killiansburg Cave Hiker Biker Overnighter, a wooded campground with bathroom facilities.

The trail passes through a pasture dotted with cedars, and cliffs rise from the other side of the river. The ruins of an old lockhouse and lock are visible near milepost 74. Spring flowers in this wooded area include bloodroot, pansy violets, meadow rue, and wild ginger.

When you see the chalets of the Bavarian Inn atop the cliffs on the West Virginia side of the Potomac, you're close to Shepherdstown, West Virginia. To reach the Mountain State's oldest town, follow the path under the highway bridge and take a paved access road uphill two-tenths of a mile past three old stone houses. There you will take the sidewalk along Route 34 over Rumsey Bridge.

This towpath stretches 184 miles along the Potomac River from Washington, D.C. to Cumberland, Maryland.

From the Rumsey Bridge, you can see the piers of several bridges wiped out in floods in the early 1900s. In June 1861, the Confederates burned a bridge at this spot. One of the Confederates, Henry Kyd Douglas, had lived on Ferry Hill Plantation (now C&O Canal National Historical Park headquarters) above the bridge. In his memoir, *I Rode with Stonewall,* Douglas described his emotions as he looked over at his home on the Maryland side, knowing his father was a stockholder in the property he was helping to destroy. "I knew I was severing all connection between me and my family and understood the sensation of one who, sitting aloft on the limb of a tree, cuts it off between him and the trunk," he wrote.

After you cross the Potomac, the Bavarian Inn is a few hundred yards on your right. In addition to the Bavarian Inn's tantalizing marinated rabbit, Wiener schnitzel, apple strudel, and American specialties, Shepherdstown offers an opera house that still shows movies, at least 30 historic buildings, and a museum commemorating James Rumsey's invention of the steamboat.

Rumsey demonstrated his invention for the first time on a stretch of the Potomac facing Shepherdstown on December 3, 1787, a full 20 years before the more famous Robert Fulton invented his steamboat. On that winter day, hundreds of spectators were astounded to see the steam-powered craft plow upstream at four miles an hour, turn around clumsily, and return. Most expected the boat to sink or burst into flames. Rumsey missed fame because he never made his invention into a commercial venture. A white monument to Rumsey towers above the Shepherdstown cliffs.

Day Two

After another hearty breakfast, slip back over the Rumsey Bridge and head east (right). A mile along the towpath (at milepost 71.4) is Packhorse Ford, used by the Confederate Army to slip out of Sharpsburg the night after the Battle of Antietam. The towpath leads through a wooded area and past several private docks in the summer community of Millers Sawmill (milepost 70.6). In another one and a half miles, you will pass Antietam Village, once a forge and ironworks employing more than 200 workers, but now only a few crumbling kilns. In a nearby field lie the remains of 500 Irish canal workers who died in the cholera epidemic of 1832 and were buried in an unmarked mass grave. The epidemic delayed canal construction for the better part of a year.

Continuing on, you pass the picturesque brick and whitewash Mountain Lockhouse near milepost 67. The path takes you through groves of silver maples and sycamores. You'll also see the leathery brown flowers of pawpaws in the spring. If you're lucky, you'll spot their green plumlike fruit in September—they taste like banana pudding.

At milepost 66, the Potomac tumbles through Hook's Falls. Canoeists skirt these rapids by riding the remains of Cow Ring Sluice, dug in 1769 along the West Virginia shore. Within a mile, you see the brick-lined arches of the Shinhan limestone kilns, where limestone was burned for plaster or fertilizer until the 1960s. Manganese was also mined at this location.

Dargan Bend Recreation Area, at milepost 65, provides a convenient resting spot with picnic tables and toilets. Mallards, green-winged teals, mergansers, and wood ducks often nest along the river near this spot.

The northern tip of the Blue Ridge Mountains dwindles down to fierce rapids in the river east of here. Landscapes become more dramatic, and the low cliffs support gardens of Dutchman's-breeches, columbines, and star-of-Bethlehem. In the wet sections of the canal, crowds of sliders (turtles) splash off the logs as you approach.

After passing the remains of limestone Locks 35 and 36, you leave the Great Valley of Maryland and its limestone topography. The sight of the Hilltop House on the ridge across the tumbling Potomac is your cue to look for the spiral staircase and pedestrian walkway along the bridge to Harpers Ferry at milepost 60.7. You will share this walkway with Appalachian Trail hikers, so look for the white blazes on the bridge. To reach Hilltop House and Briscoe House, walk across Arsenal Square to High Street, your second right, and climb one of the steepest sidewalks imaginable. For Hilltop House, take Jackson Street right to Ridge; for

Harpers Ferry is a National Historical Park commemorating abolitionist John Brown's attempt to take over the armory there.

Briscoe House, follow High for several more blocks (the street name will change to Washington).

Harpers Ferry is a National Historical Park commemorating abolitionist John Brown's attempt to liberate America's slaves and set up an independent nation. He and 21 conspirators set about doing this on October 16, 1859, by taking over the federal armory in Harpers Ferry. Ironically, they managed to kill a free black man who was walking past. The U.S. Marines under Lieutenant Colonel Robert E. Lee were summoned and succeeded in overcoming the rebels in a matter of minutes. Brown was hanged a month later. His act was a catalyst for the Civil War, which turned out to be the town's downfall. Harpers Ferry was taken more than 23 times by the two armies, and it never really recovered its population or industry after that.

Now park rangers and costumed interpreters drift through the restored and reconstructed downtown to answer questions and reenact history. The park facilities are open year-round from 8 A.M. to 5 P.M.

Ground Squirrel Holler Bed and Breakfast
Sharpsburg, Maryland

You might suspect that behind the lavender trim this is no ordinary country inn. You are right. In the parlor, a neon sculpture lights up the baby grand piano and a stuffed figure sits on a daybed holding an

Etch A Sketch. Upstairs, antique headboards and feather beds dress up the three guest rooms. Pressed tin ceilings and wood stoves give a flavor of a bygone era. A hat collection lines the hallway, and baskets of assorted shapes and sizes adorn the kitchen. Ground Squirrel Holler is a place of whimsy.

A hearty continental breakfast is served in the dining room or on a sunny deck off the barn. Ground Squirrel Holler is open Friday through Sunday only. This 1910 Victorian country inn, located on a five-acre llama farm one mile from the C&O Canal Towpath, also offers llama hikes and gourmet packed lunches.

Bavarian Inn
Shepherdstown, West Virginia

The four post-and-beam chalets across the Rumsey Bridge from the C&O Canal Towpath are your first indication that you've found a little Bavaria. As you enter the gray stone mansion to check in, you're enveloped by rich, dark hardwoods and the warm, winey scent of German food. Waiting by the dining room to greet you like friends are owners Erwin and Carol Asam, whose courtly manners complete the sensation that you have arrived in old-world Germany.

In 1977, the Asams bought the rustic inn on the banks of the Potomac and proceeded to inject the Bavarian feel of Erwin's roots into the decor and architecture of the new chalets and the lodge they built. Fresco painter Annie Stensen added her touch with a gallery of Alpine scenes on the exterior walls of the chalets.

But first of all, the Asams and their chefs began producing the exquisite German dinners that would bring people out from Washington and Baltimore. The standard menu includes popular German staples like red cabbage, herring, potato dumplings, and jaegerschnitzel—veal covered with mushrooms in a wine sauce. Quality white wine, not vinegar, adds to the rich taste of many meat dishes, and only homemade soup stocks are used.

In addition to the *geschmorte rindroulade* (a roll of roast beef stuffed with bacon and pickles), schnitzel, and other German specialties, the Bavarian Inn serves pasta dishes, shepherd's pie, and thoroughly

American dishes such as New York strip steak.

Dining is in the Hunt Room, where jackets are preferred after 5 P.M., or downstairs in the hiker-casual Rathskeller.

You have your choice of rooms here: rooms above the inn, riverfront rooms with Jacuzzis and fireplaces, garden view suites, and corner rooms with balconies. Most rooms have queen-sized canopy beds and balconies. All the fireplaces have gas logs that ignite at the flick of a switch.

Hilltop House Hotel
Harpers Ferry, West Virginia

Thomas Lovett built his first Hilltop House on a rocky bluff high above the Shenandoah and Potomac rivers in 1888. The flood of 1870 destroyed most of the town's industry and later floods periodically routed downtown residents while Lovett's Hilltop House stood firm. But Lovett, an African-American native of Harpers Ferry, was not able to prevent fires in that high, windy location. His first two hotels burned down, but he and his wife rebuilt each time. The dream of owning a hotel on this site where the martyrdom of John Brown took place was too strong to accept defeat.

This old hotel has served Mark Twain, Pearl Buck, Alexander Graham Bell, and at least five U.S. presidents, many of them during Lovett's 35 years as proprietor. It's a charming old place with creaky wooden floors and a honeycomb of unpretentious rooms that are unrivaled for the best view in town. This claim can be echoed by the Hilltop dining room and taproom.

The Hilltop House's 64 rooms range from comfortable no-frills to a penthouse Jacuzzi suite. A new motel-style lodge has been built across the street. All rooms are air-conditioned and have private baths.

The restaurant, which serves 300, retains the flavor of an old-fashioned summer resort with its piano and pump organ tucked in the corners. The summer breakfast buffet is especially popular with hikers.

Briscoe House Bed and Breakfast
Harpers Ferry, West Virginia

If you'd prefer the attention and intimacy of a small bed-and-breakfast, the 1890 Briscoe House offers charm and comfort on Washington Street (the street name changes from High Street) about a mile straight up the northwest hill from the Harpers Ferry footbridge.

The large guest rooms and downstairs dining room reflect the English influence of its owners, Jean and Lin Hale. Breakfast is British, but American country in portions, served in an antique-filled dining room.

Guest rooms have private sitting rooms, cable TV, and there is one Jacuzzi suite. Well-behaved children are welcome.

Briscoe House guests often dine at the Anvil Restaurant two blocks down the street. This is a flowers-and-white-tablecloth sort of place with specialties that include jumbo crab cakes, grilled swordfish, penne pasta with artichokes, and Kentucky Derby pie.

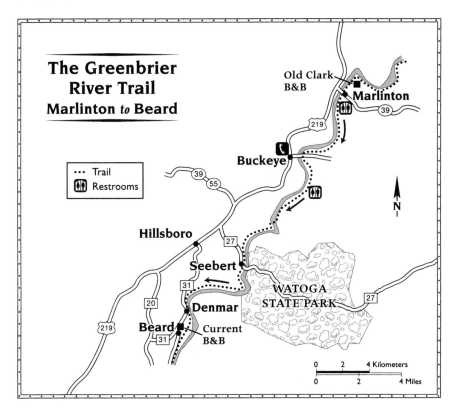

Getting there:

US 219 and Route 39 cross in Marlinton. Parking is available beside a restored train depot where the trail crosses Marlinton's Main Street, Route 39.

To get to Beard, first take US 219 north from Interstate 64 in Lewisburg or south from Marlinton, then take Route 31 east from Hillsboro for 4.9 miles to Beard Road (County Route 31/8). The Current Bed and Breakfast is within sight, and the trail is a half mile away.

The Greenbrier River Trail

Marlinton to Beard

This flat, well-groomed trail follows the Greenbrier River along an old railroad bed through hardwood forest and pastures, past the sites of several vanished logging towns.

The Lowdown

Some trails make your circulatory system scream, challenging you toward hard-won vistas until your heart throbs in your ears. Other trails pamper you, laying out their offerings—a patch of brilliant lilies, a mossy waterfall, a great blue heron on its nest—in rapid succession while you lope along comfortably with scarcely a catch in your breath. This is the nature of the Greenbrier River Trail in eastern West Virginia.

The Greenbrier River is one of the last streams in this country to flow unimpeded by dams or other man-made obstructions throughout its course. In fact, the clear waters of the Greenbrier have been consistently ranked among the state's top three smallmouth bass spots, according to the West Virginia Department of Natural Resources' trophy citation program.

West Virginians had strong economic reasons for not building dams on the Greenbrier in the 1800s. Lumbermen made massive log drives down the Greenbrier every spring from the 1870s until the railroad was built in 1900. The millions of floating pine logs scrubbed the banks clean of overhanging trees and loose rock structure, so that even today the Greenbrier's shores seem smooth and groomed. Only pines were harvested because they floated better than hardwoods. Eventually the West Virginia Pulp and Paper Company (now Westvaco) persuaded C&O to construct a railroad into the Greenbrier Valley so all the vast timber

Key at-a-Glance Information

Length: 17.5 miles

Difficulty: Easy, flat railroad bed

Elevation loss: 120 feet

Scenery: Pastures, hemlock-shaded forest, rhododendron-covered banks, and views of the Greenbrier River

Exposure: Shady–70   Exposed–30

Solitude: Some weekend bike traffic; very quiet in the spring

Surface: Packed dirt with loose gravel in a few spots; a two-mile section from Marlinton to Stillwell Park is paved

Trail markings: No markers, but well-used double track is obvious

Author's hiking time: 7 hours

Season: All seasons

Access: No permits or fees

Maps: Greenbrier River Trail maps are dispensed from Pocahontas County Visitors' Center in Marlinton's old depot.

Other uses for trail: Mountain biking, horseback riding, cross-country skiing

Facilities: Snacks and sandwiches at Jack Horner's Corner in Seebert, milepost 45.8; toilets at mileposts 55 and 50

Shuttle: Old Clark Inn owners will help you shuttle your car before your hike or take you back to your car the next morning, but you need to request this when you reserve your room. Other shuttle operators are Elk River Touring Center, (304) 572-3771; Appalachian Sport, (304) 799-4050; and Outdoor Adventures, (888) PLAY WVA.

Lodging info:

Old Clark Inn
702 Third Avenue, Marlinton, West Virginia; (304) 799-6377;
www.greenbrierrivertrail.com/rustic; $$–$$$$

The Current Bed and Breakfast, Hillsboro, West Virginia; (304) 653-4722;
www.currentbnb.com; $$–$$$

Alternative lodging:

In Marlinton, VanReenan House Bed and Breakfast (call (304) 799-6677) and Graham's Motel (call (304) 799-4291) on Route 219 a half mile from trail milepost 52. At the Seebert halfway point, there are the fully furnished Greenbrier River Cabins (call (304) 653-4646) located on the river and next to the trail. A two-night minimum stay is required.

resources here could be logged. The railroad was completed to Marlinton in October 1900, about 150 years after the brief stay of Joseph Marlin, one of the first two European settlers west of the Alleghenies and the man for whom the town was named. The Greenbrier line closed for lack of customers in late 1978.

The Greenbrier's namesake trail traces the path of the former Greenbrier division of the C&O Railroad through what was booming timber country. The trail snakes around the peaks of Marlin, Thorny Creek, and Thomas Mountains, past sleepy little villages with names such as Stony Bottom, Seebert, and Buckeye.

Marlinton's yellow and white 1901 train depot, which marks the Greenbrier Trail's crossing of Main Street, serves as the visitor's center of the Pocahontas County Tourism Commission and distributes trail maps. Stations on this line always contained an office, a waiting room, and a freight room. The traditional bay window allowed the agent to watch the tracks.

Once, Marlinton's railroad yard contained a turntable, a water tank, a trestle for loading coal, three bunkhouses, a blacksmith shop, and the section foreman's house, all needed to serve as many as 11 trains a day. Besides the depot, the only remaining railroad structures are the water tank and a concrete pump house at the north end of town. The concrete circle that marks the foundation of the turntable is visible near the water tank.

Marlinton, a town large enough to have a hospital and two stoplights, is the main metropolis on the trail. Some cyclists like to plan their rides to coincide with Marlinton's Autumn Harvest Festival in late October, although the roadkill-cookery booth set up trailside did little to tempt me. (The banter was better.)

To start your hike, go right two blocks from the Old Clark Inn to the depot, cross Marlinton's Main Street, and follow the trail (paved for the first two miles) south through the Marlinton Municipal Park. You can find water, toilets, picnic tables, and playground facilities here.

Continue on past W. M. Cramer's present-day lumberyard to the site of Stillwell, near milepost 55, where the Marlin Lumber Company built a spur up Stillhouse Run to connect with its mill. The sawmill was part of the valley's vast lumber operations built during the boom that started with the railway's completion. West Virginia Pulp and Paper Company started logging operations on Cheat Mountain at the northern end of the trail for its Covington, Virginia, mill.

Ten years after the opening of the railroad, 25 sawmills and 2 tanneries were operating along the lines. Entire new towns went up in months. But by the early 1920s, the timber in the valley was almost all cut, and whole towns just as quickly disappeared as the mills closed.

You can pick up trail maps in the restored Marlinton Depot.

At milepost 54, you can sidetrack to the Wyatt Interpretative Trail, named in honor of U.S. Forest Service employee Tom Wyatt. This short nature trail is geared toward elementary-school children but is useful for anyone who wants to know what a cucumber tree or a buckeye looks like. The trail follows part of an old railroad spur up Sunday Lick.

Back on the Greenbrier Trail, continue south as it passes through hardwood forest along the river. No trace is left of the logging villages of Aumiller and Munday Lick. The hamlet of Buckeye, located near milepost 52 on the opposite side of the river, is marked by a gauging station at the end of the blue metal bridge. You can walk the half mile over the bridge to US 219 for groceries, phone, and Graham's Motel.

For the next two miles, the trail passes through the old logging territory of the West Virginia Pulp and Paper Company, the Howard Sawmill, and the Martin Lumber Company, now reclaimed by forest. In the early mornings, you can see wood ducks and herons lifting off the Greenbrier's quiet waters. The calls of pileated woodpeckers and kingfishers ring through the woods. Bathroom facilities have recently been constructed near the mouth of Beaver Creek.

At milepost 48.1, you'll see nothing but an overgrown field on the left where the populous logging town of Watoga once stood. No sign is left of the sawmill or the kindling wood plant that operated in the early 1900s, but you can trace the foundation of the lumber company's store and see its bank vault in the brush just off the east side of the trail.

The most spectacular wreck in the history of the Greenbrier line occurred near here on May 4, 1925, when a span of the Watoga Bridge collapsed into the river. A boxcar loaded with brick derailed, slamming into the edge of the bridge and causing one span to crumple into the river. Three cars dropped with the bridge, while one remained hanging from an intact abutment. No one was badly injured in this crash and local boatmen ferried passengers across the river to the rescue cars.

In the next two miles, the trail passes first over the Greenbrier on the Watoga Bridge then over smaller tributaries on the Stamping Creek and Stephen Hole Run bridges on its way to Seebert, the halfway point. Stephen Hole Run was named for a small cave at the head of the stream that was supposed to have been home to early European settler Stephen Sewell during the winter of 1750. Sewell had shared a log cabin with Joseph Marlin, but when the two had a falling out, Sewell was rumored to have spent the winter either in the cave or in a tree trunk.

Seebert, located about ten miles from the Marlinton depot, may be the overnight destination of choice for less seasoned hikers if they can deal with the required two-night stay. Tom Cline's Greenbrier River Cabins are located at milepost 46.3 between the trail and the river. These facilities sleep from two to ten and are equipped with wood stoves, baths, cable TV, and new kitchens.

Although nothing remains of Seebert's rail facilities but the signal foundation, old photos attest to a busy station with a bunkhouse, stock pens, a section foreman's house, and sidings where lumber and coal were loaded. Seebert now serves its travelers and cabin guests with a convenience store/snack shop and bike rental operating under the name of Jack Horner's Corner. (If you are really tired of walking, you could bike the next seven miles to Beard in less than an hour.)

For the next four miles, the trail winds close to the river through old farmland and forest. The campsites of Watoga State Park are visible across the river. The park was developed by the Civilian Conservation Corps, and a small CCC museum is located there.

Bears and bobcats have been spotted on the forested section of the trail between the park and Denmar. But whether you see big game or not, you'll almost certainly see towhees, phoebes, meadowlarks, and red-wing blackbirds in the warmer months. In summer, goatsbeard, flowering raspberry, Saint-John's-wort, and milkweed bloom along the trail.

At Denmar (milepost 39.3), a multistory building rises incongruously from the fields. The former tuberculosis hospital for black West Virginians was converted to a nursing home and then to a medium-security prison. (Only one inmate has escaped in seven years, and he did not opt to spend his free time on the trail.) Denmar's medical claim to fame now is the nearby Gesundheit Institute, made famous by the 1998 movie, *Patch Adams.*

*The Greenbrier River Trail runs 76 miles from
Cass to Caldwell.*

The Denmar stop began as a sawmill and store for the Maryland Lumber Company in 1910. The name is a combination of the names of the lumber company president, J. A. Denison and the company name.

Beard (milepost 38.5), once the site of a two-story depot, a water tank, and four bunkhouses, is where you'll find your own bunkhouse, the Current Bed and Breakfast and its therapeutic hot tub. The Current is located a quarter mile down Beard Road on the right.

Old Clark Inn
Marlinton, West Virginia

The Old Clark Inn has been an inn or rooming house since it was built in 1924. But with renovations from the flood of 1996, it has gotten fancier—

offering an outdoor hot tub, two suites, and a bathroom for each of the eight bedrooms.

As soon as you spot this square brick house from the Greenbrier Trail north of the depot, you'll note the characteristic that sets it apart from most other bed-and-breakfasts—there's a swing set in the front yard. Yes, children are allowed here. In addition to the living room and dining room, the Cains have a playroom on the first floor and two resident offspring to play with guests' children.

"Our children have never met a stranger," says owner Leslie Cain. "We think this is a great way for them to grow up."

The rooms range from the Fisherman's Room on the first floor, an economical option crowded with two big beds, to the honeymoon suite upstairs. Some rooms have adjoining stall showers; others have claw-foot tubs with wraparound showers. You'll find a sink in the corner of most bedrooms—a leftover from boardinghouse days.

Cain and her husband Mike serve an ample country breakfast in the dining room or on the porch between 7 A.M. and 10 A.M. Guests can take their evening meal at the River Place Restaurant or the town diner, a few blocks away.

The Cains are an amiable couple who went into innkeeping to stay in Pocahontas County when Mike's job at the phone company was phased out. "People become self-employed to stay in West Virginia," Leslie Cain says. The nearly nonexistent crime rate, the eight nearby national forests, and the river in their backyard all make for a great lifestyle, she says, for families and for visitors.

The Current Bed and Breakfast
Hillsboro, West Virginia

Leslee McCarty has been welcoming travelers into her antique furnished, turn-of-the-century farmhouse just off the Greenbrier Trail for 15 years. She chose the name not only to reflect the river that she can sometimes hear from her patio, but for the sense of peacefulness that seems to flow in like a current in her rural community, and the connection she often feels with her guests from all parts of the world.

The Current farmhouse once belonged to the Beard family for whom the rail stop was named. The family donated land for the adjacent chapel,

which McCarty uses for parties, weddings, and overflow lodging.

Guests can choose among five comfortable double rooms and a suite with a queen-sized bed, private bath, and adjoining sitting room. McCarty will accommodate children and horses, but you'd better talk to her first before you bring your other pets. As a Humane Society foster parent, McCarty often has extra cats and dogs to give away. Be warned; some of those animals can steal your heart.

McCarty serves hearty breakfasts of quiche, French toast, fruit, and muffins in front of her large kitchen fireplace. If you're walking the trail, you'll want to make a reservation to have McCarty cook your dinner. Ask her about other attractions if you'll be extending your stay in Pocahontas County. After more than a decade on the Tourist Commission, she knows everything that is going on.

The North Bend Rail-Trail

Salem to Pennsboro

The North Bend Trail travels along the bed of an old rail line through north central West Virginia's faded industrial boomtowns. Along the way you'll see small-town life, a living history museum, a railroad museum, and a former jail interpreting incarcerated life in the 20th century.

The Lowdown

This rail-trail trip takes you through the residue of north central West Virginia's industrial history—through glass factory yards, past fields of discarded oil and gas machinery, over streams sometimes still muddy with runoff, and into faded towns built for four and five times the present population.

But this walk is not only about the past. It's a study of small towns; you pass through the beating hearts of several—Salem, Smithburg, West Union, and Pennsboro. (You can add Ellenboro and Cairo if you combine this hike with next one listed in this book.) From the backyard view, you come to know these people by the clothes on their lines, the projects on their back porches, and the signs and flags with which they mark their territory. You see them socializing and relaxing, and you marvel at how closely they live. You're seeing how small towns work.

This walk starts in Salem, a little town reminiscent of Andy Griffith's Mayberry, with knots of local walkers, porch chatters, and neighbors catching up on the news in front of the restored depot. This town is home to a small university, a restored colonial village, two festivals, and the state horseshoe championship games. Salem College (now merged with a Japanese university under the name Salem-Teikyo University) was founded in 1888 and still educates students in the liberal arts and equestrian skills.

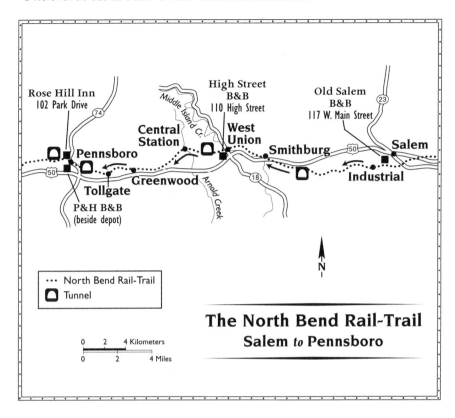

The North Bend Rail-Trail
Salem *to* Pennsboro

Getting there:

Trail access points are: Walker, Cairo, North Bend State Park, Ellenboro, Pennsboro, Greenwood, West Union, and Salem. To get to Salem, the easternmost town with lodging, take Interstate 79 to Clarksburg Exit 119 and proceed on US 50 west 12 miles to Exit 23. The Old Salem Inn is on the right side of Main Street beside the trail. West Union and Pennsboro also are located just off US 50; for Pennsboro, take Route 74 into town. P&H Bed and Breakfast is on the left over a dairy mart on the corner of 74 and Kimball Avenue. To reach the Rose Hill Inn, follow Route 74 across the North Bend Trail and turn left onto Rose Hill Road in front of Davis Handmade Marbles. The inn is a block away on the corner of Rose Hill and Park Drive.

Key at-a-Glance Information

Length: Salem to West Union: 13 miles; West Union to Pennsboro: 12 miles

Difficulty: Always flat and easy

Elevation gain: Insignificant

Scenery: Historic and cultural scenery in old towns is more striking than the natural scenery.

Exposure: Shady–40 Moderate–20 Exposed–40

Solitude: Very quiet, except around Salem in the evening

Surface: Packed dirt

Trail markings: Few, but the raised bed and path are obvious

Author's hiking time: Salem to West Union: 5 hours; West Union to Pennsboro: 4.5 hours

Season: Year-round

Access: No fees or permits

Maps: North Bend Trail map available by calling (800) CALL WVA or at North Bend State Park

Other uses for trail: Bicycling, cross-country skiing, horseback riding

Facilities: Two restaurants in Salem; pool and bathrooms at Salem Park; Smithburg General Store, 9 miles west of Salem; in West Union Cottage Corner Restaurant on Main Street and a grocery. Pennsboro has two restaurants, an IGA, and two convenience stores.

Shuttle: Rose Hill Inn in Pennsboro has a shuttle service run by a certified bicycle mechanic (call (304) 659-3488). The owner of High Street Bed and Breakfast will also shuttle his guests back to their cars.

Lodging info:

Old Salem Bed and Breakfast, 177 West Main Street
Salem, West Virginia; (304) 782-1227; $–$$

High Street Bed and Breakfast, 110 High Street
West Union, West Virginia; (304) 873-2044; $$

P&H Bed and Breakfast, 206 Kimball Avenue, Pennsboro, West Virginia; (800) 659-3241; (304) 659-3241; $

Rose Hill Inn, 102 Park Drive, Pennsboro, West Virginia; (304) 659-3488; $–$$

Demonstrating colonial crafts in Fort New Salem

The library has been open Saturdays for the last 15 years, a phenomenon that would have shocked its Seventh Day Baptist founders.

At the turn of the century Salem irritated its Seventh Day Baptists with oil-boom growth that included 13 saloons and the highest per capita income of any town in the nation. But when the town temperance union bought the newspaper in 1901, the saloons, the newspaper office, and the entire business district burned down overnight. The brick Salem you see today was built in the early 1900s.

If you are at all interested in colonial history or crafts, you should take time to visit the Fort New Salem, a short distance from Old Salem Bed and Breakfast. Go west on the North Bend Trail to the entrance of Salem-Teikyo University on Interstate 50/Route 36. Follow the entrance street past university residence halls for about a half mile, and then take Route 23/20 to the right another half mile over the mountain to the entrance to Fort New Salem.

This living-history town is a collection of relocated historic log buildings, each representing a piece of rural settlement in the area between 1792 and 1901. The original settlement was made by Scots Irish and German Seventh Day Baptists. Now part of Salem-Teikyo University, the site is peopled by costumed interpreters and artisans who give tours daily from 10 A.M. to 5 P.M. from June through October, and on weekends in April, May, November, and December. The print shop, tinsmith, and basket maker are especially popular.

To start your walk on the North Bend Trail, go straight out the front door of Old Salem Bed and Breakfast, cross Main Street, and turn right on the North Bend Trail.

Begin walking west, passing the town park with its swimming pool and horseshoe pits on the right. This area used to be called Industrial, after the state industrial school for girls up on the hill; now it's a home for troubled youth of both genders.

When you reach the shadow of Industrial Hill, you're in forest, glimpsing occasional log-camp homes and a cemetery for the Irish-American families that built the railroad. The trail continues through forest to the hamlet of Long Run, home of many Irish tunnel builders. A church and an abandoned store mark the town.

The state expects to have mile markers installed on the trail in 2001, but exactly where the numbering will start was unclear at press time. In my map, I start mileage at Wolf Summit, the easternmost terminus in 2000. For the narrative description, I will give mileage from the last town or point of interest.

You'll reach the 846-foot Sherwood Tunnel five and a half miles out of town. Set your sights on a small arc of light on the far side of the passage and watch your footing in the dim interior. Flashlights are good to have. From this point, the trail follows Buckeye Creek through a lightly wooded area surrounded by open fields.

After another three and a half miles, the town of Smithburg will come into view. Smithburg has converted its abandoned depot into a museum and memorial for the 19 souls lost when Middle Island Creek raged over its banks one night in 1950. Most of the houses on the creek side of Main Street were never replaced. Middle Island is just a small stream now, not big enough to support bass or trout.

Museum volunteer Freda Cox sometimes steps out from her home behind the general store to give personal testimony about the flood she weathered in a parked car. "The river was rising so fast, we just left dinner on the table," she says. "The next morning all the food was still there, but the water had turned the table completely around."

Besides clippings and memorabilia related to the flood, the station houses railroad relics—instructions on how to make up time for an engineer who's running late, lanterns, schedules, and recollections of the great train robbery of 1915. The mannequin operating the telegraph at the window gives you a comforting feeling, as if the past was somehow never lost, at least at the Smithburg Depot.

As you continue on your way to West Union, you cross Middle Island Creek three times in as many miles. Middle Island Creek is one of the longest creeks in the world, meandering 145 miles in the mountains to meet the Ohio River only 35 air miles from its origin. During the Civil War, Confederate raiders swooped in to destroy portions of the Union-held railway in this area. A guardhouse stood beside the easternmost bridge over Middle Island Creek.

Cross Middle Island Creek for the last time and enter West Union, once a major hub of the oil, gas, glass, and logging industries. When the trail crosses Main Street, turn left, make a quick left-hand jog onto Church Street, and then another left on Court Street to the courthouse. The town's 1899 courthouse presides over West Union like a grand cathedral. In its shadow is a must-see jail museum that will give you as realistic an experience of the county penal system as you can get without breaking the law. The jail closed in 1986; now museum volunteer Bill Calhoun will show you how little space and privacy inmates had and what it feels like to have hundreds of pounds of clanking steel gate shut you off from the outside world. The museum also houses many rooms of artifacts related to the town's commercial, military, social, and religious history. You'll wrap up the day by staying at the elegant High Street Bed and Breakfast, located across the backyard from the jail.

Day Two

After a comfortable overnight—with no nightmares of those clanking jail doors, you hope—you head north back through West Union's business section, whose tall buildings seem quiet on any day of the week. Within a few hundred yards, you're back on the trail as it crosses Main Street and parallels Garrison Avenue west out of town. The trail passes a primitive campground and picnic pavilion built for trail users. Soon you're entering the cool darkness of Central Station Tunnel, at 2,297 feet the trail's longest tunnel. The other side will appear only as a speck of brightness. A reassuring word: In three years and hundreds of tunnel crossings, North Bend Trail Association President Randy Stemple says he's never seen a snake in any of the trail's 12 tunnels.

You exit the tunnel into surreal, blazing sunlight, even if it's a cloudy day, and soon come to the ghost town of Central Station. The cluster of houses around an abandoned store doesn't look like a hangout for dangerous criminals. But in 1915, a train robbery took place near here that stumped government officials for months. The thieves hid out in the woods and went their separate ways when the heat was off. Years later all

*Mark Twain said passing through North Bend
Railroad's many tunnels was like riding
the longest subway in the world.*

of the men were apprehended with the help of a local farm girl who had
seen the men camping in a field. Jesse and Frank James also were rumored
to have hidden in Central Station after robbing a Huntington bank.

The trail continues past several "daylighted" tunnels, which look
like bare cliffs now, and through some open fields before reaching the
small towns of Duckworth and Greenwood. If you want to shorten your
trip, Greenwood offers lodging in the 1960s-style Greenwood Motel and
food at the Lone Star restaurant. Most folks, however, will want to continue on four more miles through Toll Gate and over the Hughes River to
Pennsboro.

You emerge from between steep hills into downtown Pennsboro
before you have a chance to glimpse the four-story buildings from a distance. The restored depot will be on your left and a line of shops, including Davis Handmade Marbles, on your right.

If you are staying at the P&H Bed and Breakfast, turn left on Route 74 just before the depot. The P&H and its adjoining restaurant by the same name are located on the right-hand corner of the next block. The bed-and-breakfast does not have a sign, so look for the closed dairy mart on its ground floor. If Rose Hill Bed and Breakfast is your destination, walk two blocks down the trail to the white house on the hill above the trail. Wherever you stay, make sure to take time to explore the town.

Pennsboro is another former boomtown that looks loose in its brick infrastructure. Multistory buildings surrounding Pennsboro's renovated depot now house a church, a paintball store, and a beauty shop in their lower levels. This small business district also contains junk and antique stores and a shop selling handblown marbles. Three blocks away is one of four factories in America where glass marbles are still manufactured (another lies about four miles west in the town of Lamberton). Another anachronistic attraction in Pennsboro is Harold's Olde Printery on Sand Gap Road just before a trail tunnel. Harold Shive will demonstrate his old style equipment by appointment (call (304) 659-3320).

Yet another Pennsboro attraction was here more than a century before the rail line. The old Stone House Museum building, with its rambling add-ons to the rear and its two-foot fieldstone walls to hold in the heat, is a curiosity. The original section of the house is one of the oldest in northern West Virginia and served as a stagecoach stop that accommodated Stonewall Jackson and Sam Houston. The museum contains at least nine rooms of artifacts donated by Doddridge County citizens—boxes of rhinestone jewelry, military uniforms, needlework, furniture, and an oil-based hair tonic produced locally by a failed oil speculator. Although the museum board has never heard of any lawsuits from the hair tonic, they admit smoking must have been risky with a well-oiled "do." The museum is open by appointment (call (304) 659-2384).

Across from the Stone House is a field of discarded oil and gas equipment owned by the Mountain State Oil and Gas Historical Association. Just down the road, at the Pennsboro Speedway, stock cars compete in the Hillbilly 100 in early September and the Dirt Track World Championship on the third weekend in October.

Old Salem Bed and Breakfast
Salem, West Virginia

This 100-year-old home sits in the heart of Andy Griffithsville. Salem is a small town where folks can catch up with their neighbors while walking the North Bend Trail. You can watch the social interchange of a small town in action from Old Salem's front porch; the trail passes by, running parallel to Main Street. From the back deck, you can check up on the wood-chucks and gardens.

The Old Salem was built by the first president of Salem College and is now jointly owned by retired college adminis-trator Evert Pearcy and Alice Proper, his caretaker. A more than hospitable hostess, Proper washed our hiking clothes, offered us the use of her car, and invited us down to the TV room for evening snacks.

"I want you to feel like this is your home," she urged. "My favorite guests take over the house. It's wonderful." And she was not being sarcastic.

But after dinner (either across Main Street or two miles west on Main at Corner Cottage Too), we're content to lie on the deck's twin recliners and watch the sun go down over the neighborhood gardens. Besides a suite, there are two other bedrooms that share a bath and an upstairs TV lounge. The furnishings are a comfortable mixture of modern pieces and antiques.

Breakfast is served in the formal dining room at whatever time guests request. A former restaurateur, Proper knows how to make fluffy bis-cuits, great eggs any style, and hearty country breakfast fare. If you make the request ahead, she'll pack you a lunch to go.

High Street Bed and Breakfast
West Union, West Virginia

This 1906 Queen Anne house is the fanci-est bed-and-breakfast on the trail, with its exquisite iron fireplace covers, oak woodwork, and spacious rooms. Paul and Liz Jerrett spent two years renovating the Victorian house. The Jerretts are a family of craft hobbyists who relocated from Pennsylvania to demonstrate black-smithing, tinsmithing, and other crafts at Fort New Salem on weekends.

The home features a modern kitchen, carefully collected West Virginia antiques, four guest rooms, and attractive flower gardens. Reservations must be made at least two days in advance.

The High Street is directly across the backyard from the jail museum in West Union.

P&H Bed and Breakfast
Pennsboro, West Virginia

This attractive one-room bed-and-breakfast is located over an old dairy mart beside the P&H Family Restaurant in downtown Pennsboro. It is cozy, seemingly in the center of things, and yet strangely quiet at night in this semi-ghost-town business district. The apartment has tasteful modern upholstered furniture and a comfortable queen bed.

For evening entertainment, there's television and the church next door. Or else you can take a walk. The carpet rolls up early here, unless there's a race at the Pennsboro Speedway.

In the morning, you go downstairs to the P&H Restaurant (the P&H stands for Pennsboro and Harrisville Railroad line) and choose from a variety of breakfast offerings—the omelets are great. The railroad decor is friendly and so is the staff, if they aren't too busy with breakfast regulars.

Rose Hill Inn
Pennsboro, West Virginia

Originally built around 1860, the Rose Hill overlooks the trail just a block from the P&H and offers a few more rooms (four). The common area features a comfortable front porch overlooking the trail, a sunroom/gift shop,

a library, and an open porch bordered by a rose garden.

The owners' qualifications to serve trail guests are superb; John Schaffer is a certified bike mechanic, and his wife, Donna, is a nutritionist. They run a deli on the side. The Schaffers will shuttle guests and non-guests for a fee.

The North Bend Rail-Trail

Pennsboro to Cairo

This section of West Virginia's North Bend Trail passes through wild and natural areas and beside the outdoor kilns of a marble factory, several glass-outlet stores, and a stagecoach inn, as well as North Bend State Park.

The Lowdown

The 72-mile-long North Bend Trail makes up one link in the 5,500-mile American Discovery Trail that stretches across the country, but the North Bend Trail is a relatively undiscovered link. It is also the only section through West Virginia that offers conveniently spaced lodging facilities in combination with an off-road path. For a four-day walking trip, you can combine this hike with the Salem-Pennsboro trek.

Before you begin your hike, you might want to explore Pennsboro. Once a booming oil and gas town, Pennsboro now looks loose in its multistory brick downtown. The trail passes a renovated depot and a small business section with junk and antiques stores, as well as an outlet for handblown marbles. If you are interested in the history of printing, you can visit Harold's Olde Printery on Sand Gap Road near the trail tunnel for a demonstration of old style equipment (call (304) 659-3320).

As the trail leaves town heading west, it passes near the backyard of the old Stone House Museum, with its two-foot fieldstone walls. The original section of the house, one of the oldest in northern West Virginia, served as a stagecoach stop that lodged Stonewall Jackson, Sam Houston, and others. The museum contains at least nine rooms of artifacts donated by Ritchie County citizens—boxes of rhinestone jewelry, military uniforms, needlework, furniture, and an oil-based hair tonic produced locally by Harry Lambert, a failed oil speculator. Lambert, who lived just down the trail, maintained a mansion, an airplane, and West Virginia's largest swimming pool, so when his oil drilling started coming up dry, he

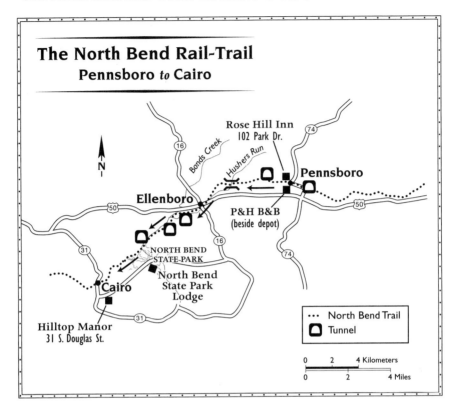

Getting there:

Trail access points are: Pennsboro, Ellenboro, North Bend State Park, and Cairo.

To reach Pennsboro, take Route 74 right off US 50 into town. P&H Bed and Breakfast is on the left over a dairy mart on the corner of 74 and Kimball Avenue. To reach the Rose Hill Inn, follow Route 74 across the trail and turn left onto Rose Hill Road in front of Davis Handmade Marbles. The inn is a block away on the corner of Rose Hill and Park Drive.

To reach the Hilltop Manor in Cairo from US 50, take Route 31 south three miles to Douglas Street (there will be a sign here for Hilltop Manor) and go left up the hill to the yellow and white house.

Key at-a-Glance Information

Length: Pennsboro to North Bend State Park Lodge: 11.5 miles; North Bend State Park Lodge to Cairo: 5.1 miles

Difficulty: Always flat and easy

Elevation gain: Insignificant

Scenery: Historic and cultural scenery in old towns and industrial sites is more striking than natural scenery, except near North Bend State Park

Exposure: Shady–60 Moderate–20 Exposed–20

Solitude: Quiet, except for weekend bicycle traffic near the state park

Surface: Packed dirt

Trail markings: Few, but the raised bed and path are obvious

Author's hiking time: Pennsboro to North Bend State Park Lodge: 5 hours; North Bend State Park Lodge to Cairo: 2.5 hours

Season: Year-round

Access: No fees or permits

Maps: North Bend Trail map available by calling (800) CALL WVA or at North Bend State Park

Other uses for trail: Bicycling, cross-country skiing, horseback riding

Facilities: Two restaurants and three groceries at Pennsboro; Dairy Queen at Ellenboro, 5 miles from Pennsboro; bathroom facilities, pool, and dining at North Bend State Park; Village Inn restaurant, convenience store, and bike shop at Cairo

Shuttle: Rose Hill Inn in Pennsboro has a shuttle service run by a certified bicycle mechanic (call (304) 659-3488); $–$$.

Lodging info:

P&H Bed and Breakfast, Pennsboro, West Virginia
(800) 659-3241 or (304) 659-3241; $

Rose Hill Inn, 102 Park Drive,
Pennsboro, West Virginia; (304) 659-3488; $–$$

North Bend State Park, Cairo, West Virginia, (304) 643-2931 or (800) CALL WVA; $–$$ (meals extra)

Hilltop Manor Bed and Breakfast,
31 South Douglas Street, Cairo, West Virginia; (304) 628-3711; $

The Stone House Museum in Pennsboro began life as a stage coach inn.

cast around for other moneymaking schemes. The tonic never caught on in a big way, probably saving him from lawsuits by smokers who ignited their oily heads.

If you are a race car fan, you might check out the stock car races at the Pennsboro Speedway, just down the road. The Hillbilly 100 is held in early September and the Dirt Track World Championship takes place on the third weekend in October.

Once you have finished exploring, head west out of Pennsboro on the North Bend Trail through a lightly forested area and over Husher's Run Bridge. In three and a half miles, you'll reach Lamberton, named for the millionaire who tried to market petroleum hair products. Lambert made his short-lived fortune around 1898 and built the state's first air-field near here.

Although you won't see any active oil derricks along the trail, the glass industry is still alive and glowing in outdoor kilns on the right side of the trail at Lamberton. As the trail becomes more popular, I hope hikers will still be able to watch marbles rolling out of the red-hot ovens at Mid-Atlantic Glass. The kilns operate continuously, casting their rosy glow along the trail late at night. The company, one of West Virginia's oldest glass factories, specializes in handblown glass in the plant on the left side of the trail. The gift shop is open weekdays all day from 9 A.M. to 5 P.M. and Saturday from 9 A.M. to 2 P.M.

Another glass outlet, West Virginia Glass Specialty, is located one and a half miles down the trail near the Ellenboro (pronounced Ellen-burr) bridge. It is open Monday through Friday from 8 A.M. to 4 P.M. and Saturday from 9 A.M. to 4 P.M. The arched railway bridge over Route 16 provides the only climbing you'll do on the whole trail. Look below for a Dairy Queen bumped up against an old church. It will be your last chance for refreshments until North Bend Lodge.

After Ellenboro, the trail viewscape widens and becomes more scenic, following Husher's Run's pools and rapids through a mature forest for five miles. You can spot deer on the other side of the creek and occasionally foxes, rabbits, and squirrels. Deep pools of still, black water breed tadpoles. Picnic tables and benches sit at regular intervals in this model section of trail. The first tunnel in this section, known as Old Tunnel Number 10, is short but pretty. It is the only one of the trail's tunnels constructed entirely of raw, carved rock and is depicted in the North Bend Trail Association's logo. The next tunnel, almost two miles later, reveals scrapes left on its ceiling by train cars as they got larger over the years. Bond's Creek Tunnel, in another half mile, marks the entrance to North Bend State Park. Look for the sign and a dirt path to the park on the left.

The trail and the state park get their name from the horseshoe curve in the North Fork of the Hughes River. The 1,400-acre park once contained quarries, lumber mills, and oil and gas wells, whose remains can still be seen along the trails. To reach the lodge, leave the North Bend Trail to follow the small trail on the left for about a mile to the first pavilion, then go past an amphitheater, turning right at a bridge toward the campground. Go up the steep road for another mile past the pool to a mini-golf course and lodge on the ridge.

The park is open year-round, although the campgrounds close for winter. The lodge offers 29 guest rooms with air conditioning and satellite television. Park amenities include tennis, mini-golf, swimming pool, a restaurant, and a gift shop offering West Virginia crafts.

Day Two

After breakfast at the lodge, retrace your steps out to the North Bend Trail at Bond's Creek Tunnel. Head west (left) through the town of Cornwallis, if you notice it. The town's sparse houses separated by brush no longer look like a neighborhood that deserves a name. It is located just west of the park trail.

A Union blockhouse once stood here as defense against marauding Confederate guerrilla forces. In 1900, oil derricks covered every hillside in the area, but recently the wooden structures were removed as safety hazards. Sandstone quarries just west of Cornwallis were prized for their bridge-building stone.

All five of the tunnels between Cornwallis and Cairo (pronounced Ker-o) have been blasted open for easier passage. The tunnel two and a half miles east of Bond's Tunnel was attacked and its cribbing was burned by Confederate raiders during the Civil War. Some of the guerrillas in this rebel raid were women dressed in men's clothing.

The trail crosses over the North Fork of the Hughes three times and then pushes into Cairo. Some of Cairo's three- and four-story buildings still stand, but their upper stories are empty. Now the 500-person town supports the Country Roads bike shop, a restaurant, a grocery, an antique but fully functional post office, and a hardware store. The hardware store is a unique, turn-of-the-century mercantile, with windup toys for adults, old-fashioned tools, and a miniature oil drilling operation in the window.

This is a short day. You may want to continue on to Silver Run Tunnel, two more miles west, site of an annual ghost story-telling and hollering contest. You just might find someone practicing the bloodcurdling yell or the diabolical laugh. For unique events like this one, Cairo has been named the festival town of West Virginia.

P&H Bed and Breakfast
Pennsboro, West Virginia

This attractive one-room bed-and-breakfast is located over a former dairy mart beside the P&H Family Restaurant in downtown Pennsboro. It is cozy, seemingly in the center of things, and yet strangely quiet at night.

For evening entertainment, there's cable television and a church next door that hosts an event almost every evening. Or you can hang out at the P&H Restaurant (open until 7:30 P.M.) or at Roberto's pizza parlor down the street (open until 10 P.M.). The carpet rolls up early here, unless there's a race at the Pennsboro Speedway.

For breakfast, you go downstairs to the P&H Restaurant (the P&H stands for Pennsboro and Harrisville Railroad line) and select any item on the menu—the omelets are great. The railroad decor is friendly and so is the staff, if they aren't crazy busy with regulars who drive up to 25 miles to breakfast here.

Rose Hill Inn
Pennsboro, West Virginia

The Rose Hill overlooks the trail just a block from the P&H and offers a few more rooms (four). The common area features a comfortable front porch overlooking the trail, a library, a gift shop, and an open porch bordered by a rose garden. A carryout deli has been added, and plans are underway for an outdoor pool.

The owners' qualifications to serve guests on this trail are superb: John Schaffer is a certified bike mechanic with a good supply of bike parts, and his wife Donna is a nutritionist. The Schaffers will shuttle guests and non-guests for a fee.

North Bend State Park Lodge
near Cairo, West Virginia

North Bend Lodge features 29 spacious guest rooms (there's one suite and a room with a waterbed) with a view. Each room is equipped with two

double beds, a private bath, air conditioning, satellite television, and a telephone. The lodge also features West Virginia handmade oak furnishings and a homey sitting room with a central fireplace. The gift shop sells West Virginia products, and the dining room serves three meals a day.

Hilltop Manor Bed and Breakfast
Cairo, West Virginia

Guests at the Hilltop Manor have a special treat at breakfast—proprietress Marianne Cullings' rendition of southern gospel favorites. The

professional musician might even throw in a few tunes from the 1930s and 1940s for an appreciative audience. And for those who heap on the compliments, she may haul out her guitar or banjo.

This is not what you expect from someone with a Brooklyn accent. Cullings and her husband, Robert, searched the Appalachians nine years ago for a place to retire and run a bed-and-breakfast. They chose Cairo for its tranquillity, friendly people, and mountain scenery.

"There's not a window in any of our guest rooms that doesn't have a view of mountains and trees," Cullings says. "It's so quiet up here that you can hear birds and crickets."

Hilltop Manor offers five comfortably furnished and modestly priced guest rooms with queen- or king-sized beds and three shared bathrooms. The downstairs of this plain Victorian home is furnished mainly in oak with cabinets displaying the Cullings's collections of antique toy cars and music boxes. Although the establishment doesn't accommodate children or pets, it does provide games for adults—croquet, badminton, and horseshoes—as well as television in the living room.

Breakfast is ample; Marianne considers it a challenge to fill you up to the point where you won't need lunch. A typical spread includes an omelet made with vegetables from the Cullings's garden, hash browns, homemade muffins and jam, fruit compote, juice, and coffee.

Hilltop Manor doesn't serve dinner, but meals are available at the Village Inn in downtown Cairo, five blocks away.

Snowshoe Mountain Hut Hiking

This hike starts from a ridge-top resort city with spectacular views and amenities and follows a trail deep into a spruce forest to a rustic, staffed cabin accessible only by foot and all-terrain vehicles.

The Lowdown

Some great hiking can be found in places you wouldn't naturally associate with backcountry wilderness. West Virginia's Snowshoe Mountain Resort, for instance.

After a recent investment of $62 million, this major southern ski resort is beginning to look like a small city. The resort now contains 15 restaurants, 10 retail shops, and housing for more than 3,000 guests. But Snowshoe owns 11,000 acres, 90 percent of them undeveloped forest. Some 120 miles of hiking and mountain biking trails wind over old logging roads through Cheat Mountain's spruce, pine, and yellow birch.

Although all your hiking on this expedition takes place in one resort, you are probably traveling through wilder, more divergent territory than on almost any other hike in this book. It is not unusual to hear a bobcat scream in the spring or see owls or raptors from the cabin porch.

This hike goes to Sunrise Backcountry Hut, built in the fall of 1999 out of local timber. This rustic but aesthetically furnished lodge sits on a ledge overlooking the eastern Alleghenies three miles distant from the main resort, serving those who seek the backcountry experience away from paved roads and public utilities. An additional cabin will be constructed on the same trail further out in the backcountry near Shavers Lake in summer 2001.

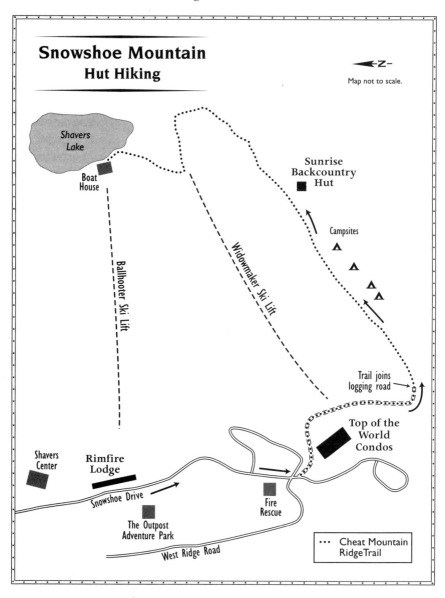

Getting there:

From the south, exit Interstate 64 at White Sulphur Springs, then take Route 92 north for about 50 miles. North of Dunmore, take Route 66 west about 15 miles through Cass to Snowshoe. You will see the large Snowshoe Resort sign and welcome center on the right, just before the Inn at Snowshoe. Turn right onto Snowshoe Drive (County Road 3) and head up

Getting there (continued):

Cheat Mountain three miles to Snowshoe Village. Brigham (where you check in) and Rimfire Lodge are on your left.

From the north, exit Interstate 79 at Weston and drive to Elkins on US 33, then go south 43 miles on curvy US 219 to Route 66 on the left. The sign and welcome center for Snowshoe Mountain Resort are on your left in a half mile.

Key at-a-Glance Information

Length: Rimfire Lodge to Sunrise Backcountry Hut: 3 miles (optional additional hike to Ballhooter ski lift: 4 more miles)

Difficulty: Mostly downhill going to the cabin, moderately strenuous returning to the mountaintop

Elevation loss: 1000+ feet

Scenery: Thick spruce forest, with views of wilderness

Exposure: Shady–80 Moderate–5 Exposed–20

Solitude: Perfect

Surface: Packed dirt and logging road that stays muddy after a rain

Trail markings: Fairly well blazed

Author's hiking time: 1 hour down; 2 hours back

Season: Year-round; snowshoeing, snowmobiling, cross-country skiing in the winter

Access: Must be a Snowshoe Mountain Resort guest

Maps: Snowshoe Mountain Resort biking map

Other uses for trail: Mountain biking, snowshoeing, cross-country skiing, and snowmobiling; also used by the resort's all-terrain vehicle

Facilities: None on trail, but food and bathrooms at Snowshoe Village and the Boathouse near Ballhooter lift; outdoor and indoor bathrooms at Sunrise Backcountry Hut

Shuttle: You can walk out the way you came, walk downhill to the ski lift June–March, or ride on the resort's all-terrain vehicle.

Lodging info:

Sunrise Backcountry Hut at Snowshoe Mountain Resort
Snowshoe, West Virginia; (304) 572-5252; www.snowshoemtn.com;
$$$–$$$$ per person (includes breakfast and dinner)

Rimfire Lodge at Snowshoe Mountain Resort
Snowshoe, West Virginia (304) 572-5252; www.snowshoemtn.com;
$$–$$$$$ (meals extra)

Snowshoe Resort's Cheat Mountain Ridge Trail leads into bear country.

To get there from the top of Snowshoe Mountain, take Snowshoe Drive right from the Outpost Adventure Park a quarter mile uphill to the trailhead for the Cheat Mountain Ridge Trail. You'll see the trailhead on the left, just past the Shavers Fork Fire and Rescue Station and across from the intersection with South West Ridge Road.

The trail passes by the Top of the World condominiums and drops over the mountain under the Widowmaker lift. You enter the dark, spruce forest on a stony path through hay-scented ferns and wild shamrocks. Here and there a bright fire cherry adds its flamboyant color to the mix. Goosefoot maple, Eastern hemlocks, and yellow birch also put in frequent appearances at this altitude. If you ever find yourself trying to start a fire in rain or snow, remember that the high oil content of the yellow birch bark makes it excellent kindling.

Mother Nature dumps almost twice as much rain on 4,848-foot Cheat Mountain as it does on the ridges only 20 miles to the south, so you'll see a big difference in the types of mosses, ferns, and lichens up here. The thick lichen cover on tree trunks and rocks indicates good air quality. Look on old logs for the green Dixie cup formations so prevalent up here.

You also will probably see signs of bears. Black bears leave their mark on Cheat Mountain, mostly in paw prints and strewn garbage they salvaged from resort dumpsters, but you may also see the typical berry-filled bear scat. A bear encounter is unlikely, and in most encounters the bear wanders away.

Should you meet a black bear—even a cub—on the trail, most experts recommend you back away slowly, staying close to the others in your group and speaking in a soft monotone. Don't turn your back and run away from the bear—that's acting too much like prey, and the bear is more likely to pursue you. And bears are faster than you. Keep calm, avoid direct eye contact, and never turn your back. If a bear charges, stand your ground; bears sometimes "bluff charge" several times before leaving. Don't play dead because black bears have no qualms about chewing on carrion.

However, none of this is likely to happen. Only 23 people have been killed by black bears in the past century in North America. You are 180 times more likely to be killed by a bee. Farther out, you may see the large pad print of a bobcat or even a mountain lion. Snowshoe naturalists say the mountain lion's retractable claws identify the big cat's prints; other animals show claw prints. On spring nights, you could hear the bobcat's cry, a shriek that sounds like a woman in pain.

After three-quarters of a mile, the trail joins an old logging road. Although the forest is lush and thick on Cheat, it was logged extensively in the early part of the century. Hikers can still discover parts of old winches and other logging equipment in the forest.

Follow the logging path as it plunges down the mountain, through several low boggy spots, and up a small incline before passing five primitive campsites on the ridge. Most of these spots feature tent platforms, and all have gorgeous views of Pocahontas County.

Sunrise Backcountry Hut is located at least a half mile beyond Bear Claw, the last campsite, on a ledge overlooking a vast ripple of Pocahontas County forest. Solar-powered lights make a path through the spruce to the bathhouse.

For those desiring an extended hike (seven miles total, out and back from the lodge), the trail continues beyond the cabin another three miles to the bottom of Ballhooter ski lift, offering more opportunities to glimpse hawks, foxes, and deer. This trail is more narrow, marked in orange ribbons as it leads to a fire tower. Before reaching the tower, however, you will take a left turn and follow the steep, pink-ribbon-blazed extension of Cheat Mountain Ridge Trail through the perpetual night of dense spruce thickets and along a small stream to Widowmaker lift. This descent takes about an hour from the hut and sees some weekend bike traffic.

Widowmaker only operates in the winter. A mile down the double track forest road straight in front of you is Ballhooter lift, which runs daily in summer and fall to take guests to Shavers Lake.

In 2000, the resort built a beach on the western shore of Shavers Lake, about 20 yards from the base of the Ballhooter lift. The lift transports guests to the waterfront (and hikers and bikers back to the mountaintop). You will need to ask for a lift ticket at registration. The Boathouse restaurant at the lake serves waffles, sandwiches, and salads. A concession for canoes, paddleboats, and windsurfing offers many options for getting into the water.

So, in summer, fall, and winter you have the choice of returning to the summit of Cheat on the Cheat Mountain Ridge Trail or hiking downhill to Shavers Lake for the lift. In any season, you can be shuttled from the cabin on the resort's six-wheeled all-terrain vehicle; simply request the shuttle when you make your reservation.

Rimfire Lodge at the top pampers you with its patio hot tubs, private whirlpool tubs, gas log fireplaces, coffee house, and chocolate shop. In the winter, you'll appreciate the basement parking garage.

Sunrise Backcountry Hut at Snowshoe Mountain Resort
Snowshoe, West Virginia

Sunrise Hut sits on a ledge overlooking a sea of trees for miles and miles. No passable access road or utility line exists within three miles of the

cabin, yet cabin guests hardly have the sense of roughing it. Not in this whistle-clean cabin where the guide cooks up a hearty, four-course meal on the bottled gas range.

Though bathroom facilities include a solar shower that few will attempt in winter, this is a more luxurious version of the New England hut-to-hut experience. At Sunrise, guests have indoor bathrooms with hot and cold water and privacy in separate rooms or curtained beds. The guide, who's part storyteller, part historian, and part chef, sets up lanterns throughout the common living room/dining room area. Rooms are gently illuminated with lamps powered by wind-generated, 12-volt electricity. No sleeping bags are necessary here; the hand-tooled log beds are spread with thick comforters and extra blankets.

From the A-frame hut's porch, you'll probably hear wildlife you barely recognize—the shriek of a golden eagle, a barred owl's hoot, perhaps a fox in breeding season, and warblers of diverse types.

"I think people can have many levels of appreciation for the place, from the sunrise to the owls to the social experience to the knowledge of how lightly we're treading on the landscape here," says Steve Rice, the former Snowshoe general manager who conceived the idea for Sunrise.

Trash is buried or packed out. Rainwater slides off the roof into a collection area for washing dishes. The hut's spruce and pine siding and some of the interior beams were cut on Cheat Mountain and milled in Pocahontas County.

Meals amply repay your efforts in reaching Sunrise Cabin. The dinner always includes bread freshly baked in the cabin as well as "just desserts." Guests can choose ahead between vegetarian or meat entrees. The guide has breakfast waiting in the morning to provide fuel for the hike out.

An especially popular way to enjoy the Sunrise Hut is to participate in a guided night hike to the spot. Wildlife is more active in the thick spruce forest at night, as is your imagination—especially with the guide's evocative stories.

Rimfire Lodge
Snowshoe, West Virginia

Rimfire Lodge, at the top of Snowshoe Mountain, can be the start or end of your expedition. It is the other extreme from the rustic Sunrise Hut. Rimfire has a city feel, with its underground parking, adjacent shops, and nearby courtyard of restaurants.

But this little city has an unsurpassed view of the mountain forest, which is especially enjoyable from the two outdoor hot tubs on the second-floor deck. The spacious lobby features a large fireplace, whose gas flames may be crackling on summer evenings when temperatures sometimes dip into the 40s. The twig chairs are rustic and comfortable thanks to an Appalachian upholsterer from North Carolina.

Rimfire's modern suites have one or two bedrooms, some with kitchens. But cooking will probably be the last thing on your mind when you can go downstairs to experience a variety of prepared cuisines. All rooms are climate controlled, with the standard cable television and in-room phones.

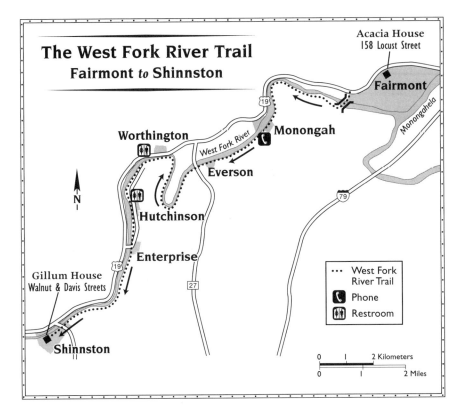

The West Fork River Trail
Fairmont *to* Shinnston

Acacia House
158 Locust Street

Fairmont

Monongah

Worthington

West Fork River

Everson

N

Hutchinson

Enterprise

Gillum House
Walnut & Davis Streets

Shinnston

··· West Fork
River Trail

Phone

Restroom

0   1   2 Kilometers
0   1   2 Miles

Getting there:

From Interstate 79, take Exit 137 into Fairmont and follow Route 19 south (Locust Avenue) through town. Acacia House is on Locust, after the street turns left and goes up a hill two blocks from downtown.

Shinnston is located 16 miles down the trail or 11 miles south on Route 19. Gillum House is two blocks from the Route 19 bridge, at the corner of Davis and Walnut Streets.

The West Fork River Trail

Fairmont to Shinnston

This scenic rail-trail runs through a forest that is reclaiming the land between northern West Virginia's coal and oil towns along the West Fork River.

The Lowdown

This walk is partly about natural beauty, partly about man's savage attack on the land in pursuit of coal, oil, and gas. Now the railroad is gone, most of the factories lie in ruins, rust-colored water seeps from the mines, and nature persists. The wounds of the earth have been bound and covered over with honeysuckle and spring beauty. The towns seem quiet and pensive, as if reflecting on their earlier industry.

The trail officially begins to the north of the 510-foot Fairmont trestle, within a one and a half mile walk from Acacia House along two-lane Locust Avenue. To get there, go left on Locust Avenue to Country Club Avenue, turn left, and go one block. If you are driving, park at the Shop 'n Save lot and walk down Edgeway Drive to Joyanne Street where you will descend to the river on a steep, gravel alley. The cinder path at the bottom officially becomes the West Fork River Trail in two-tenths of a mile when you cross over the West Fork on the bridge. From the bench on the southeast side of the river, you can make a mile detour to use the bathrooms and park facilities at Mary Lou Retton Park.

The West Fork River Trail abruptly turns into a nature park, with wooded hills so thick with spring beauty in April that the earth seems to quiver with nodding pink flowers. Dutchman's-breeches, white trillium, and blue river phlox add accents in mid-spring.

Key at-a-Glance Information

Length: 16.5 miles

Difficulty: Always flat and easy

Elevation gain: Insignificant

Scenery: Turn-of-the-century mining and oil towns, as well as waterfalls, secluded forest, wildlife, and river views

Exposure: Shady–10 Moderate–30 Exposed–60

Solitude: Fairly quiet; volunteer bicycle patrol checks the trail daily

Surface: Two lanes of packed dirt and cinders

Trail markings: At road intersections, but the double-track path is well worn and obvious

Author's hiking time: 6.5 hours

Season: Year-round

Access: No fees or permits

Maps: West Fork River Trail map available through Marion County Parks and Recreation Commission, P.O. Box 1258, 316 Monroe Street, Fairmont, West Virginia 26554; (304) 363-7037

Other uses for trail: Mountain biking, cross-country skiing, horseback riding

Facilities: Drink machine and telephone at Monongah; drinks at Everson; bathrooms and snacks at Worthington; toilet at Hutchinson

Shuttle: Acacia House and Gillum House will help their guests shuttle luggage and vehicles between the inns. The two bed-and-breakfasts have a package arrangement that includes lodging, breakfasts, dinner, picnic lunch, and shuttle for an extremely reasonable price.

Lodging info:

Acacia House, 158 Locust Avenue, Fairmont, West Virginia; (888) 269-9541; www.callwva.com/gillum; acacia@acaciahousewv.com; $–$$

Gillum House, 35 Walnut Street, Shinnston, West Virginia; (888) 592-0177; www.acaciahousewv.com; gillum@citynet.net; $–$$

The West Fork River Trail follows an old rail line through former industrial towns and forests.

The small streams you see flowing out of the woods are the color of orange soda, probably due to acid mine drainage. The coal causes the water to have a low pH, which makes the iron tailings in the rocks precipitate out and give the water its rusty appearance. No tadpoles were swimming in the swill, but the surrounding vegetation was lush.

The cluster of houses near the trailhead is called Norway. Businesses on the opposite side of the river face Route 19, their backsides turned toward the West Fork. But mostly, you are alone with the crows, the ducks, and the great blue herons. Every mile or so you can rest your legs on one of the considerately placed benches.

In three miles, you approach the warehouse and rusted machinery of the Consolidated Coal Company. On the opposite side of the trail is a ballpark with a bathroom and bleachers. This is the outskirts of Monongah, a town whose main claim to fame came in 1907 when the local Fairmont Coal Company's mine exploded, killing 362 men and boys. Congress reacted to the disaster by toughening mining laws, but in 1968, another explosion less than a mile from Monongah killed 78 men at the Consul Number 9 mines.

A small monument in front of the town water office, a block south of the trail, is the only reminder of the 1907 tragedy that claimed every man in some Monongah families. The turn-of-the-century brick downtown section is crumbling, and the Levy building no longer inhabited. A pool hall is one of the few remaining businesses that continues to operate. The grocery sits vacant, but you can still buy cold drinks at the machine beside the fire hall and use the phone at the police station to summon a shuttle from the bed-and-breakfasts if you decide to end your hike here.

Not that quitting would be a good idea, with so much remaining to be seen. The Monongah bridge reveals a pretty stretch of river, as well as a distant junkyard high on a mountain. Ignore that. You'll find your treasures here in close-up views, like the colonies of Virginia bluebells and the brick beehive-shaped coke ovens on the left of the trail. Red trillium, larkspur, and dogtooth violets add to the wildflower mix on the left bank.

As you continue on, you'll see traces of old mines and mining roads. In two miles, the trail passes a home store offering juice, water, and T-shirts at the crossroads of Everson. Be careful crossing busy Route 27 near milepost 9. (Mileage is measured from Shinnston.)

The trail chases the river around a horseshoe curve for three miles from Everson to Worthington. Seven small waterfalls splash down the bank toward the trail; most of the water is clear. In the summer, a cooling shower here would be very tempting.

After the tip of the curve, signs of turkey, deer, and other wildlife become common as the land opens up. The concrete foundation of several buildings and the outskirts of Worthington come into view just before the trail makes a sharp bend around a steep hill. From the river, Worthington is a pretty little town with houses lined along the shore and an old school high on the hill. Worthington has dammed the West Fork for swimming and fishing. Worthington Park is the only spot on the trail offering flush toilets, running water, and picnic tables. You can watch softball and horseshoe games in the park from benches placed along the trail.

If you take a small detour across the bridge into downtown Worthington, you can pick up snacks and Amish food at the R Corner convenience store or buy groceries and meat sandwiches at Demus Market.

The trail continues south along the wooded riverbank seven-tenths of a mile to the remains of a yellow brick industrial building and the company town of Hutchinson. If you need to sit, look for a ball field just beyond a small playground. When no game is in session, you can rest in the shaded dugout. A port-a-potty sits behind the dugout.

Just beyond Hutchinson is a forest honeycombed with ATV trails. Be alert here. The vehicles are likely to catapult into the West Fork Trail to turn around.

Shortly after Hutchinson, you pass from Marion to Harrison County. Look for brick coke ovens where coal was processed along the tracks on the left as you come into Enterprise, another company town of identical duplexes. A sheltered bench at the center of town provides a good place to relax if the resident chow dog decides you pass the scent test.

*Effluvium stripes rock ledges along
the West Fork River Trail.*

In the three miles from Enterprise to Shinnston, the trail passes rock cliffs striped by multicolored effluvium. The effect of the red, orange, and chalky white striations is as lovely as the Petrified Forest in Arizona, but the dead grasses in the flow line seem ominous.

Your first glimpse of Shinnston is a large, pretty house jutting out from a clover-green hill. As you round the curve, you see the brick warehouses and the Route 19 bridge.

The town was laid out in 1815, when commerce revolved around its gristmills and sawmills. The B&O Railroad came to town in 1890 to take out the coal mined nearby. Within two decades, oil and gas wells were the major economic activities in town. Energy continues to be the main employer, but now it is the North Harrison Power Station, whose smoke stacks loom over town.

Shinnston seems poised to serve a whole county's snacking needs with two ice cream places, three pizza parlors, a sub shop, and several restaurants. A unique town feature is the Eucharistic Perpetual Adoration

Chapel, a small, unmarked brick building where people of all faiths can go for prayer any hour of the day or night.

The trail continues through town, passing Gillum House on Walnut and Davis Streets and crossing over the Richardson Trestle to end at Ferguson Park.

Acacia House
Fairmont, West Virginia

Fairmont is a city of magnificent buildings constructed during the first two decades of the century. The High Gate Mansion, the "Million-Dollar" Monongahela Bridge, the ornate Marion County Courthouse, and Saint Peter the Fisherman Catholic Church with its Australian glass windows

are just a few of the National Historic Register buildings that make the city's walking tour a worthy warm-up for the West Fork hike.

The sturdy, brick Acacia House fits right in with Fairmont's celebration of the past. The four-story brick house, with its high windows and elegantly carpeted floors, was built in 1917 for architect T. L. Burchinal, who designed the Marion County Courthouse a few blocks away. The home features oak woodwork, six decorative gas fireplaces, and a glass-enclosed front porch from which to watch town life go by.

The bed and breakfast glitters with collectibles. Kathy Sprowls, who runs the inn with her husband George, sells antiques at three regional antique malls. Acacia House's gift shop is her fourth outlet. If you want to take home a truly unique gift from your travels, this is the place to shop. But making up your mind can take time; the store is filled with a myriad of glassware, jewelry, salt shakers, pottery, and other small collectibles.

The Sprowls' own enviable collections of plates, pillboxes, finials (the decorative tips of lamps), and other items are displayed in cases, shelves, and cabinets in the living room and dining room. These items can halt progress toward the tempting breakfast, so be sure to look them over when you check in.

The spacious Evergreen and Rose rooms have their own adjoining bathrooms, while the Dogwood Room shares a bath with those who occupy the twin beds of the Maple Room. Guests can relax in front of the wood-burning stove in the TV room or take their afternoon refreshments on the porch.

The West Fork Package with Gillum House includes two nights' stay, dinner, lunch, two breakfasts, and shuttle at an extremely economical price.

Gillum House
Shinnston, West Virginia

Walking the 16-mile West Fork River Trail and staying at Kathleen Panek's Gillum House could be part of a health-spa experience—except that her fat-free, sugarless muffins, breads, entrees, and desserts invite you to eat a little too much. Panek flavors her meals healthfully with homemade apple-sauce and herbs grown in her dooryard. Special dietary re-quests are her delight—with six kids and a husband living with diabetes, she's had a lot of practice.

The Panek's 1917 Gillum House was the home of the last B&O Railroad station-master in Shinnston, who later became the town mayor. City council meetings were sometimes held in the dining room of this house. Following partially in his footsteps, Kathleen Panek served on the Shinnston Town Council and has been a supporter of the extension of the West Fork Trail.

Trail hikers enjoy extra touches at Gillum House—cut flowers in their rooms, a basket of fruit on the dresser, and a fragrant soak in the claw-foot bathtub with its brass handheld shower. All three of Gillum House's bedrooms share the bathroom; a chamber pot is located under each bed for emergencies.

The largest room, the Gillum Room, has a queen-sized poster bed with a pillow-top mattress and satin comforter. The decor includes Victorian dolls, model train cars, and a kerosene lamp. The Harris Room features a reading nook with a rocker and books that you can take home with you. No need to spend your vacation with your nose in a book.

The last room, Rosi's Room, is named after an earlier family's daugh-ter. Here, teenage Rosi once scribbled her loves' names on the wall by her bed. The Windsor-style double bed is covered with a down-filled com-forter and flannel sheets in cooler weather. The paintings in the rooms were created by host John Panek, who is locally famous for his portrayal of a colonial frontiersman at the nearby 1778 Levi Shinn log home.

Both Gillum House and Acacia House have made arrangements for a local masseuse to give massages in-house for a reasonable fee. With a few days' notice, you can also rent bikes from the Marion County Parks and Recreation Department. They will deliver mountain bikes and helmets to either establishment for rental at $8 a day.

Virginia Hikes

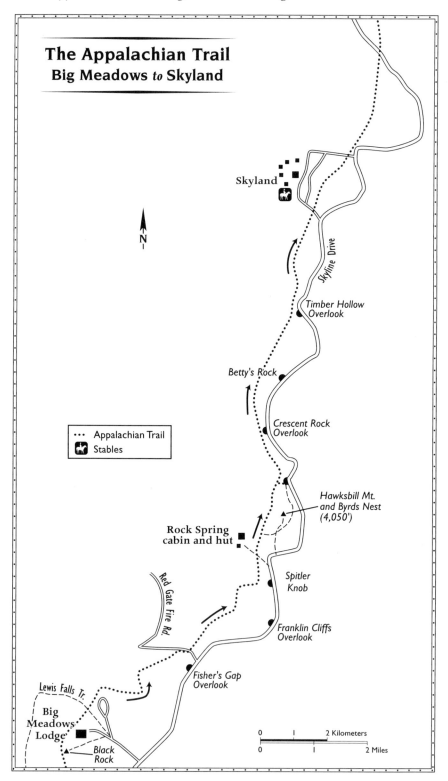

The Appalachian Trail
Big Meadows *to* Skyland

Skyland

N

Skyline Drive

Timber Hollow
Overlook

Betty's Rock

··· Appalachian Trail

Stables

Crescent Rock
Overlook

Hawksbill Mt.
and Byrds Nest
(4,050')

Rock Spring
cabin and hut

Spitler
Knob

Red Gate Fire Rd.

Franklin Cliffs
Overlook

Fisher's Gap
Overlook

Lewis Falls Tr.

Big
Meadows
Lodge

Black
Rock

0   1   2 Kilometers

0   1   2 Miles

The Appalachian Trail

Big Meadows to Skyland

Walk the Appalachian Trail along the Blue Ridge crest as it winds through central Shenandoah National Park. The park's highest peak and views of Shenandoah Valley underscore the natural beauty of this hike.

The Lowdown

Shenandoah National Park is a rugged place. One look at the gnarled, stunted, even skeletal trees up on the ridge tops should give anyone a clue: life is not easy at the heights. Some of the richest soils have washed away, and the prevailing winds slam time and again against the slopes that face west. Storms frequently strike the ridge, and park employees tell of lightning hopping from rock to rock in the stony soil. So be aware of the weather when you start out on this hike. Storms sweep up suddenly. And there's nothing secure about negotiating your way through a forest of dead and damaged trees during a high wind. But spend any length of time here, and you will appreciate those who had the forethought to set this land aside as a national park.

Sixty-five years ago when Shenandoah National Park was formed, there were few trees and no deer in this part of the Blue Ridge Mountains. The trees had been timbered and the deer had been hunted out of existence. After the park was created in 1936, a dozen white-tailed deer were introduced. With no one to hunt them and few predators, the deer went forth and multiplied. Today there are 5,000 deer in the park, and they own it. The deer seem almost insolent in their claim to the trails and roadways. You nod at them and step to the side around them. The land was left to heal itself, and today you can see how quickly much of the forest has recovered.

Key at-a-Glance Information

Length: 8.8 miles

Difficulty: Fairly strenuous, especially the side trail to Hawksbill

Elevation gain and loss: 1,150 feet

Scenery: Spectacular views of western Page Valley and Massanutten Valley

Exposure: Shady–80   Moderate–10   Exposed–10

Solitude: Busy around lodges and Hawksbill in summer, but some stretches are quiet, especially on weekdays

Surface: Dirt

Trail markings: White blazes

Author's hiking time: 5 hours

Season: Spring through fall; winter conditions quickly become treacherous, and the road is not cleared of snow

Access: Fee for car to enter Skyline Drive

Maps: Shenandoah National Park Service map of Skyland and Big Meadows Trail available at visitors centers; *Appalachian Trail Guide to Shenandoah National Park* available through Appalachian Trail Conference

Other uses for trail: Hiking only

Facilities: None, except at Big Meadows and Skyland

Shuttle: Skyland and Big Meadows lodges can contact Park Service rangers for shuttle when rangers are traveling between lodges.

Note: For the budding naturalists or adults who forgot their binoculars, Explore Backpacks containing field guides, hand lenses, and binoculars can be rented for $5 a day at park visitors' centers.

Lodging info:

Big Meadows Lodge; $$–$$$$ (milepost 51.3 on Skyline Drive), Skyland; $–$$$$ (milepost 41.7 on Skyline Drive)

To make reservations for either, call ARAMARK Virginia Sky-Line Company at (800) 999-4714 or visit the Web site at www.visitshenandoah.com

Getting there:

To get to Big Meadows Lodge, get on Skyline Drive at Thornton Gap (mile 31.5), accessible via US 211 between New Market and Warrenton, and head south.

The Shenandoah National Park section of the Appalachian Trail offers frequent vistas of Page Valley.

Despite the fact that Shenandoah is only a mile or two wide in most places, it is remarkably rich in wildlife. Rangers say that bobcats, foxes, beavers, skunks, raccoons, flying squirrels, and bears live here, although most of these animals forage at night when visitors don't see them. Park officials say that Shenandoah has the highest density of black bears of any park in the world—one per square mile—but some park employees have never seen one. Apparently, the bruins are much less curious about human beings than vice versa.

To get from Big Meadows to Skyland, you will follow part of the famous, 2,100-mile-long Appalachian Trail (AT). From Big Meadows, go left from the front door of the main lodge to meet the Lewis Falls Trail as it parallels the driveway. Turn left on this trail, following it down to the amphitheater. The white-blazed AT crosses behind the stage. Turn right to follow the AT through scrubby oak, laurel, and quartz-veined boulders and over Monkey Head Knob. You'll be hiking along the edge of Big Meadows Campground. Openings in the forest reveal fine views of Hawksbill and Stony Man Mountains to the northwest.

The trail starts to descend, passing small David Springs on the left. On the way down, look for the southernmost stand of northern gray birches. You pass over a rivulet twice and along a neighborhood of boulders the size of houses. As you walk, notice the colonies of hemlocks. Their days are numbered. The tiny hemlock woolly adelgid is already sucking sap from the flat needles of these evergreens, withdrawing needed nutrients and water. After a few years of this, the trees lose most of their needles and die. Hemlocks everywhere are being killed by this nasty import from Asia. The National Park Service cannot afford to spray all the trees, but it hopes some will develop a natural resistance to the pest. Meanwhile, the loss of the hemlocks will be hard on the brook trout and the red squirrels, which live in the trees' dense shade.

A mile and a half past the starting point, you pass a short spur trail up to the Fishers Gap Overlook and an intersection with the Red Gate Fire Road. This gap is the route General Stonewall Jackson took in November 1862, when he led 25,000 Confederate troops from Antietam, Maryland, to Fredericksburg, Virginia, to help General Robert E. Lee repel a federal attack on Richmond. Jackson was known as wily and unpredictable because he was always marching his troops long distances over the Shenandoah watershed to launch surprise attacks.

A quarter mile past the fire road, the trail passes a post marking a spur trail to Franklin Cliffs. The trail continues below the cliffs, which were formed by a prehistoric lava flow. Splinters of the basalt composite rock add splashes of gray-green along the path, but the pink mountain laurel will likely divert most hikers' attention through the late spring.

In a mile and a half, a spur trail leads a few hundred feet uphill to the Spitler Knoll parking overlook. The trail levels off and passes an old road before starting a gentle descent. At about three and a half miles into the hike, the AT crosses a spur trail leading to the Rock Spring Hut, for use by AT thru-hikers, and Rock Spring Cabin, a locked facility rented through the Potomac Appalachian Trail Club. Just past this area, the remnants of an old orchard are barely visible among young pine and locust trees.

In a third of a mile, you'll see the Salamander Trail (no name sign), a spur to the right that leads nine-tenths of a mile to the 4,050-foot summit of Hawksbill Mountain. Leave the AT for the time being and take this steeper trail as it winds around the mountain, being careful to look out for rattlesnakes in the talus slope. These steep cliffs are also home to the rare Shenandoah salamander. The red spruce, alder, gray birch, and stunted oak at this elevation make this area look more like Canada than Virginia.

Before reaching the overlook at the top, the trail passes the Byrd's Nest Number 2 picnic shelter. The stone observation tower gives excellent views of Timber Hollow to the north and Page Valley to the west. In the summer of 1989 and 1990, a pair of peregrine falcons was reintroduced to the park here. They nested and returned annually until 1999, when the female disappeared. Park officials are hoping the male will return with a new mate. On unusually clear days, you can see the skyline of Washington, D.C., from here.

Take the Lower Hawksbill Trail nine-tenths of a mile down to the northern Hawksbill Parking Area where it joins the Appalachian Trail. In a third of a mile, the trail passes under the cliffs of Crescent Rock—more eroded remnants of an ancient lava flow. Small streams falling through mossy cracks in this rock create one of the most magical spots on the hike. You can hear the tinkle several hundred feet down the trail. The stones are so metallic they clink like money under your feet. The boulders jumbled together below the eroded cliffs seem on the verge of moving again, but the trees growing up among them are evidence of their immobility.

In a mile, you come to an open area, where a spur trail leads to the Timber Hollow Overlook on Skyline Drive. For a while, the AT travels parallel to the road, but it is shrouded by a mountain laurel thicket. The trail then moves away, ascending to 3,560-foot Pollock Knob for good views back to Hawksbill Mountain and Ida Valley. If there is any wind at all, it will roar over the ridge here like Class V rapids on a plunging river.

The stone reinforcements along the trail here and at other spots were created in the 1930s by the Civilian Conservation Corps, President Franklin Roosevelt's army of the unemployed. Ten CCC camps worked nine years in the park to control soil erosion, plant trees, build stone bridges, construct campgrounds, improve trails, and erect rock guard-walls along the Skyline Drive.

From here the trail ascends slightly, then follows the horse pasture fence to Skyland stables. Pass them and take the paved Skyland Road left to the lodge.

Skyland
Shenandoah National Park

Skyland (at milepost 41.7 on Skyline Drive) was originally established as a private resort in 1888 by George Freeman Pollock. His father, with the help of investors from Boston and Washington, purchased 5,371 acres of mountain land to mine copper from the Stony Man Mountain. When the mine played out in 1850, the land sat idle. Then in the fall of 1886, 16-year-old George Freeman fell in love with the scenic area and told his dad he wanted to build a rustic resort there. George Pollock Sr. and 2 other investors backed George Jr.'s idea. In the next two years, the teenage Freeman showed the land to at least 20 prospective buyers and collected more than $3,000 in sales. He and

his partners borrowed money to build a lumber mill to provide materials for Skyland cabins. Unfortunately, those first cabins burned down.

By 1902, Freeman had fully developed the resort. More than 50 bark-covered cabins had been constructed, as well as a communal dining hall, a recreation building, tennis courts, and a private gas plant.

When the national park was established in 1936, most of the buildings were renovated and kept in use. In fact, 15 historic structures and part of Pollack's landscaping can still be seen at Skyland. You can still rent Byrd's Nest and other original cabins with fireplaces and kitchenettes, but modern suites and motel style lodging are also available among Skyland's 177 units. All Skyland lodging is being renovated with a Roaring Twenties theme that harkens back to the wild parties Pollack was rumored to have thrown during the Prohibition.

Hungry hikers can find the park's specialty, blackberry ice cream pie topped with meringue and blackberry syrup, at both Skyland and Big Meadows. The dining rooms in both these facilities also offer three meals a day, featuring regional cuisine such as mountain trout and country ham. Taprooms at both facilities refresh their guests with "mountain drinks" and summer nightly entertainment of folk and bluegrass music. Hikers can order box lunches at the restaurants.

Skyland's facilities are open from late March through early November.

Big Meadows Lodge
Shenandoah National Park

If you appreciate the diversity of nature, you'll especially like your stay at Big Meadows. A family of bobwhite quail call out their name on summer evenings in the nearby sunny, open meadow where visitors can see strawberries, blueberries, and huckleberries as well as a host of wildflowers. Behind the cabin area on Black Rock, you can watch the raptor migration from late August through October.

Big Meadows Lodge was built in 1939 by the Civilian Conservation Corps using native chestnut salvaged after the chestnut blight and stones cut from Massanutten Mountain. In 2000, the lodge was reroofed with tiles handcrafted to resemble the original stone shingles ordered by

Richmond architect Marcellus Wright Jr. It is listed on the National Register of Historic Places.

The 20 alcove rooms upstairs in the main lodge smell of distant campfires and the pine that panels the ceilings and walls. Accommodations in the other 72 rooms range from rustic cabins to multi-unit buildings with modern suites and breath-stopping views of Page Valley.

Big Meadows is open from mid-May through October.

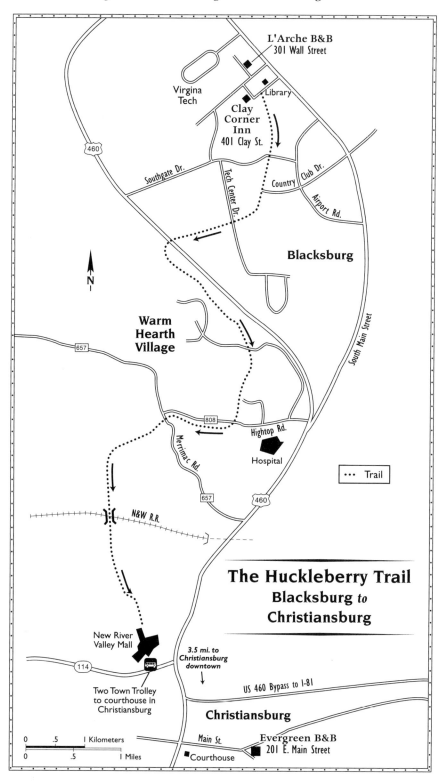

L'Arche B&B
301 Wall Street

Virgina
Tech

Library

Clay
Corner
Inn
401 Clay St.

460

Southgate Dr.

Tech Center Dr.

Country Club Dr.

Airport Rd.

Blacksburg

↑
N

**Warm
Hearth
Village**

657

South Main Street

808

Hightop Rd.

Merrimac Rd.

Hospital

657

460

N&W R.R.

···· Trail

The Huckleberry Trail
Blacksburg *to*
Christiansburg

New River
Valley Mall

114

*3.5 mi. to
Christiansburg
downtown*
↓

US 460 Bypass to I-81

Two Town Trolley
to courthouse in
Christiansburg

Christiansburg

Main St.

Evergreen B&B
201 E. Main Street

■ Courthouse

0   .5   1 Kilometers
0   .5   1 Miles

The Huckleberry Trail

Blacksburg to Christiansburg

Walk the Huckleberry Trail as it meanders past Virginia Tech farmland, wooded areas, a retirement village, and a historical coal-mine park, ending at a shopping mall.

The Lowdown

The Huckleberry Railroad Line started, like many enterprises in the area, as a gleam in the eye of a Virginia Tech professor. Mechanical engineering department head L. S. Randolph decided in 1901 it was high time to build a railroad from Christiansburg to Blacksburg, a trip his students had to make by horse and buggy over a rutted road. Of course, a stop at the Merrimac coal mine would make the venture lucrative.

The tracks reached Merrimac in 1902 and Blacksburg in September 1904, just in time to save incoming students the hack ride. Because there was a single track and meager switching facilities in Blacksburg, the engine would reconnect in front of the trailing cars at the line's terminus and back up all the way to Christiansburg.

Passengers often disembarked several times before reaching their destination—once in Merrimac when coal cars were added and whenever the locomotive would stall on a grade. When this happened in the summer, they would pick huckleberries from bushes along the tracks, hence the name.

The train could make the trip to Christiansburg in 40 minutes, but that seldom happened. Virginia Polytechnic Institute (now called Virginia Tech) cadets would say that they could step off the moving train to pick a bucketful of huckleberries without fear of being left behind. The jokes got worse; one cadet suggested that the cowcatcher be moved from the

Key at-a-Glance Information

Length: 6 miles

Difficulty: An easy 1 to 3 percent grade, with three hilly exceptions

Elevation gain: Negligible

Scenery: Pasture, woods, and views of Virginia Tech

Exposure: Shady–20   Moderate–20   Exposed–60

Solitude: Fairly well used, except midday on weekdays

Surface: Asphalt

Trail markings: At crossings and mileposts

Author's hiking time: 3 hours plus 15-minute bus ride to downtown Christiansburg

Season: Year-round

Access: No permits or fees

Maps: On signposts at ends and Warm Hearth, Merrimac, and Richard Talbot pocket parks

Other uses for trail: Biking, rollerblading, cross-country skiing

Facilities: None except at termini; bathrooms at mall and Blacksburg library

Shuttle: Blacksburg Transit's Two Town Trolley stops at the Blacksburg downtown post office, New River Valley Mall, and the Christiansburg courthouse (see www.btransit.org or call (540) 961-1185). The innkeepers at L'Arche, Clay Corner, and the Evergreen can often shuttle guests, but you must make these arrangements with your reservation.

Lodging info:

L'Arche Bed and Breakfast, 301 Wall Street, Blacksburg, Virginia (540) 951-1808; $$$–$$$$

Clay Corner Inn, 401 Clay Street SW, Blacksburg, Virginia (540) 953-2604; www.claycorner.com; claycorner@aol.com; $$–$$$

Evergreen Bed and Breakfast, 201 East Main Street, Christiansburg, Virginia; (540) 382-7372; www.evergreen-bnv.com; $$$–$$$$$

Alternative lodging:

In Blacksburg, Virginia Tech–run Donaldson Brown Hotel and Conference Center (call (540) 231-8000) is three blocks from the trail. In Christiansburg, the elegant Oaks Victorian Inn (call (540) 381-1500) is four blocks east of the courthouse on Main Street, and the Budget Inn (call (540) 382-6625) is three blocks west of the courthouse on Main.

The Huckleberry leads along Virginia Tech farmland and through private forests.

front of the locomotive to the back of the last coach to prevent cows from overtaking the train.

The train and most of the huckleberries are gone now, but blackberries and black raspberries do still grow in profusion along the trail as it enters university property near Talbot Park.

The Huckleberry Trail leaves Blacksburg from the Blacksburg library parking lot, at the corner of Miller Street and Preston Avenue. To

Getting there:

To get to the Evergreen, take Exit 118 off Interstate 81 to Christiansburg and follow US 460 West into downtown. Turn right on Main Street and go just past the Episcopal Church to the Evergreen, on the right.

To get to L'Arche, take US 460 to Blacksburg's Southgate Drive (Virginia 314). Turn left at the first intersection onto Duck Pond Drive and turn right at the top of the hill onto Washington Street. Pass the Virginia Tech dormitories and go through the four-way stop at Kent Street, taking the next left on Otey Street. L'Arche is on your left at the corner of Otey and Wall Streets.

To reach Clay Corner, follow the above directions to L'Arche, but turn right at the four-way stop onto Kent Street. You will see the main house of Clay Corner Inn almost directly in front of you at the stop sign on Clay Street.

get there from L'Arche, turn left in front of the house on Wall Street, walking toward Virginia Tech, then turn left on Kent Street. Walk up the hill and across Washington Street, then turn left where Kent dead-ends into Clay Street. (Pick up the walk here if you stayed at the Clay Corner Inn.) Continue for about 100 feet, then turn right onto Harrell Street. The Huckleberry Trail begins on the left and continues past one of the town's oldest neighborhoods on the left and a community that is evolving into student housing on the right. Once Tech employees lived on Warren and Harrell Streets behind Lane Stadium, but now students pay twice as much rent for a house split into three apartments. So the Pentecostal Holiness Church on Warren Street looks forlornly out at a neighborhood of residents under 25 who usually sleep in Sunday mornings.

At the time the railroad began, the university's commencement would draw visitors from across the state. People would start pouring into town the day before graduation, and many would camp in tents and wagons along the roads and on campus. The attraction was not the graduation ceremonies themselves, but the ensuing sham battles in which V.P.I. cadets would reenact Civil War battles. Occasionally the victors of these battles were not those recorded in history.

Tall hardwoods draped with bittersweet and honeysuckle now shade the Huckleberry Trail through the area near campus. Songbirds flit across the path, and you'll see an occasional rabbit or raccoon only four blocks from downtown.

The trail passes over Southgate Drive on a small bridge and continues past the Virginia Tech turf farm (on the left), where researchers experiment with varieties of grass that require less mowing and can take more use. On the right is the manor house of the Tech German Club, a fraternity that has planned Tech's formal dances since waltzes were popular.

At the Richard Talbot pocket park, walkers can choose to double back to Blacksburg on the Country Club Drive extension trail up to Airport Road and Gables Shopping Centers or they can continue on the Huckleberry Trail. The small park offers a rest break at its gazebo and benches. Talbot was the first dean and driving force behind the Virginia-Maryland College of Veterinary Medicine, located a quarter mile away.

The trail continues along a hedge of chokecherries and blackberries, turning sharply to the right at the boundary of the Virginia Tech Airport. Although the old Huckleberry Line continued straight, the trail now detours up a small incline and over a field in the Tech dairy farm, affording walkers a panoramic view of Tech's Lane Stadium and Cassell Coliseum.

At the top of the hill, the trail crosses over Tech Center Drive (watch for traffic) and dips through a pasture to an oak grove. A paved path parallel to the street leads out to Tech's Corporate Research Center and the airport. Walkers may notice white patches on the rumps of the Holsteins pasturing here, part of an experiment on the fertility cycle of dairy cows.

Huckleberry Trail milepost

After winding through a parklike stand of old oaks at the top of the next hill, the trail passes under an overpass built for farm vehicles and descends another small slope, turning sharply to the left to pass under US 460. Watch out for cyclists at this blind corner.

The trail turns sharply to the left again and ascends to a bench overlooking Tech's pasture and no-till cornfields. The trail is shielded from US 460 by a hedge of autumn olive and honeysuckle, with an occasional poison ivy vine adding another layer of impenetrability.

As you continue on this trail past milepost 2, you'll see a few of Warm Hearth retirement community's wooden condominiums on the eastern edge of Tech's fields. The retirement village is about 70 percent wooded, and trails wind among the condominiums, apartments, and assisted living units. One trail leaves the village driveway about 50 yards from its intersection with the Huckleberry Trail. To make a side trip on this small trail, get permission and maps from the recreation center in Warm Hearth's apartment area. A few benches, a Huckleberry Trail map, and a small flower garden mark the Warm Hearth pocket park.

The trail crosses Hightop Road past milepost 3, a fairly busy county road leading to Montgomery Regional Hospital. The trail meanders through woods on the opposite side of the road, playing tag with Lick Run. This is the flower garden of the trail; spring varieties include Bowman's root, wild geranium, columbine, fire pinks, anemones, and white clintonia. This area was the repository of trash for years, but thanks to numerous "Bloomin' and Groomin'" cleanups, the only clue to the past is a rusted can or bedspring twisted into folk art.

In a quarter mile, the trail crosses Merrimac Road, another busy byway, and traverses a concrete bridge into an open area along a stream. This stretch of the trail once passed the Merrimac and Brumfield coal mines and the town that grew up beside them. No trace of the company town on the right slope remains, but the mine that fueled the Confederate ironclad, *Merrimac*, in the Civil War is represented by a rusted winch, a collapsed mining shaft, and piles of coal on the left. Sometimes as many as 200 men were employed hauling hard coal out of Price Mountain. The Merrimac mine was flooded when it was finally closed after unresolved strikes in 1935. The Brumfield mine closed a few months after a methane explosion killed six men in 1938.

On the right, you'll see signs marking the sites of the company store, houses, and a spring named for one of the miners, as well as occasional puddles of orange water leaching out from the exposed coal. The county and several Radford University students created the mining-history interpretive park you'll see on this stretch of path.

The trail crosses a gravel road and a bridge and traverses a trestle over an active Norfolk and Western railroad line. The live tracks emerge from a tunnel on the left. On the opposite side of the bridge is an iron and wood pagoda built for trail users by the town of Christiansburg.

The steep cliffs along the trail once echoed with train whistles, as the locomotive approached Peppers Ferry Road. Soon the trail passes Corning Glass property and the landscape opens into swamp and pasture. You'll see New River Valley Mall, the southern terminus of the trail, up ahead. You can go straight to the theater entrance (where the bike racks are), get a bite at the food court, watch a matinee, or go directly through the mall to its main entrance. Here you can catch the Two Town Trolley to the Christiansburg courthouse on the hour, from 11 A.M. to 6 P.M., except on Sundays during the summer. This progressive bus system features racks to carry bicycles.

To get to the Evergreen Bed and Breakfast, walk two blocks left of the courthouse (northeast) on Main Street. The backyard pool will be waiting.

L'Arche Bed and Breakfast
Blacksburg, Virginia

Vera Good calls her 1903 Federalist Revival–style home "Charlottesville West" because of the elegant touches added in the last half century by a former owner who claimed direct lineage from Thomas Jefferson. The columns on the front porch, the Chippendale fences, and the rotunda-style gazebo all add a new dimension of style to the unpretentious home built on a hill beside what was once a small, spartan military college.

L'Arche's five comfortable guest rooms are decorated with stylish comforters or handmade quilts and period antiques. Two rooms have extra beds to accommodate children over 12. Special features are a Delft-tile fireplace and canopy bed in the Blue Room, a grand piano in the living room, a wide porch overlooking the Virginia Tech campus, and a formal tea garden.

High tea is served by reservation from 3 P.M. to 5 P.M. weekdays in the garden, the cavernous dining room, or on the tea porch. Good makes all her own pastries, cakes, cookies, and sandwiches from scratch and offers more than a dozen flavors of exotic teas and coffees. Sometimes she is assisted by her mother, Vera Senior.

Breakfast, included in the room fee, is always an event. The inn serves fresh fruit, home-baked breads, coffeecake, scones, and an entree, such as individually baked eggs in Havarti cheese. Good will also prepare boxed lunches for the trail, if given a few days' notice.

Clay Corner Inn
Blacksburg, Virginia

Clay Corner is a cluster of houses with 12 guest rooms next to the Virginia Tech campus. Its Huckleberry House sits a scant 90 feet from the trail. The inn features sumptuous breakfasts with homemade cereals and a hot entree, as well as a heated swimming pool and hot tub. The pool lifeguard, a yellow Labrador retriever named Solomon, is also an author. His book, *Observations of an Innkeeper Dog*, is due out in 2001. We can't wait to hear what secrets he'll reveal.

Each of the inn's guest rooms has a private bathroom, cable TV, telephone, and king- or queen-size bed. The rooms are tastefully decorated with local art and equipped with a hair dryer, writing table, iron, ironing board, ceiling fan, and extra blanket.

The main house and twin guest houses have central heat and air conditioning. The Dogwood and Magnolia houses each offer two guest rooms, one two-bedroom suite, a kitchen, dining area, and living room. The four Huckleberry House guest rooms feature upscale decor on local themes and each has private telephone data port lines, as well as individual climate controls. A small kitchen and a living room are available to Huckleberry House guests.

Evergreen Bed and Breakfast
Christiansburg, Virginia

The blend of Montgomery County native Barbara Bell-Capozzi's southern hospitality and her husband Rocco's informal friendliness, honed in an upstate New York Italian family, are an important element of the Evergreen's charm.

The Godiva chocolates, European coffees, secluded pool, *Gone with the Wind* bedrooms, and the concert grand piano that invites you to impersonate Liberace don't hurt either. Nor do the country breakfasts that include fresh fruit, homemade biscuits, local jam, cheese grits, eggs, pancakes, and pork chops, country ham, or potato casserole. Sometimes you even get dessert.

If you ask the Bell-Capozzis what guests like best about their stay, they'll answer "sleep." The rambling, 17-room mansion, located on a hill just two blocks from Christiansburg's courthouse, is quiet enough, but the secret may be in the beds. "We've had thousands of guests, and very few fail to comment on how well they slept," Rocco says. "They've even ordered mattresses from the store where we got ours. But the secret is probably that Barbara irons all the sheets."

"It makes them smooth and comfy," she says.

Each of the five guest rooms is unique. Two have been informally dubbed the *Gone with the Wind* rooms: one features a king-size canopy bed and original copies of Margaret Mitchell's book on the night stand, and the other is the home of Rhett Beartler and Scarlett O'Beara, 2 of almost 100 Very Important Bears (collectible teddy bears fashioned for historical figures) that give the house a cozy feel.

Room 3 is a delight for the child in any adult (real children aren't accommodated here). Decorated in cheerful primary colors, it serves as stable for a working dime-store rocking horse and as roundhouse for a large die-cast metal train.

Barbara's collections are spread around the four-story house: English vases, blue and white porcelain, paper dolls, and works by local artists, as well as prints of Christiansburg scenes by the famous folk artist Lewis Miller. "The nice thing about having a B and B," says Barbara, "is that now my collections are 'decor,' not just 'stuff.'"

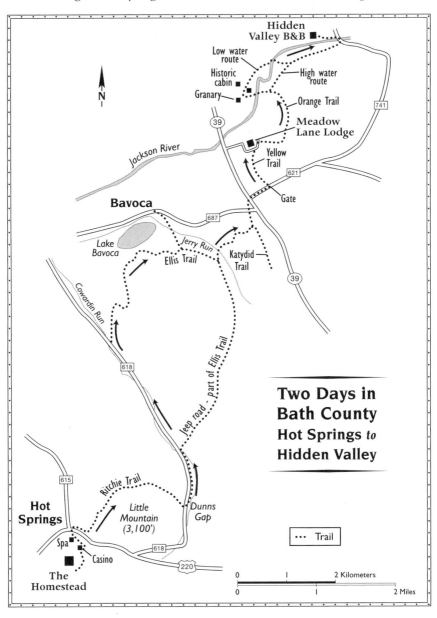

Hidden
Valley B&B ■ ......

Low water
route

Historic
cabin ■   High water
                route

Granary ■   Orange Trail

39   Meadow
            Lane Lodge

Jackson River   Yellow
                        Trail

                        621

Bavoca   Gate

                687

Lake   Jerry Run
Bavoca   Katydid
    Ellis Trail   Trail

                        39

Cowardin Run

                Jeep road – part of Ellis Trail

        618

**Two Days in
Bath County**
Hot Springs *to*
Hidden Valley

Ritchie Trail

**Hot
Springs**   *Little
            Mountain
            (3,100')*   *Dunns
                        Gap*

Spa ■   618
        Casino
**The
Homestead**   220

| 0 | | 1 | | 2 Kilometers |
| 0 | | 1 | | 2 Miles |

| ··· | Trail |

Two Days in Bath County

Hot Springs to Meadow Lane to Hidden Valley

This two-day ramble over old foxhunting trails connects a grand resort with an elegant antebellum mansion. Along the way, experience the historic grounds of a country inn with colonial roots.

The Lowdown

As I moved through Bath County's cooling forest in autumn, I was aware of the ending of a cycle. Many of the individual plants and bugs blooming and shrilling around me would not see spring. The predator birds swooping in the updraft lived a precarious existence, exchanging another creature's life for one more day of their own. Not pleasant thoughts, and yet here they seemed only part of the poignant beauty of life. The earth's energy keeps pushing through; the cycle goes on. The moment is enough in this spot of forest. I store up impressions as ransom against harder, drier times to come.

These quiet trails through Bath County's old limestone topography seem to impart a serenity that settles over you on this two-day trek. It doesn't hurt that you start at one of Virginia's premier resorts. To use the Homestead's trails, you need to be a Homestead guest. If that means you're entitled to afternoon tea in the Great Hall, a soak in the 104-degree hot pool, and a chocolate on your counterpane at night, you can handle it. Your first day of rambling will be your hardest.

Start your hike on the blue-blazed Ritchie Trail, which you can catch by walking down from the back of the main lodge to the hot baths and crossing US 220 to the paved path that goes up the hill beside Sam Sneed's Tavern. In a few hundred yards, you will reach the remnants of an old

Key at-a-Glance Information

Length: Homestead to Meadow Lane Lodge: 9 miles; Meadow Lane Lodge to Hidden Valley Bed and Breakfast: 4.5 miles

Difficulty: Moderate to difficult; at present you have to ford the cobbled Jackson River and walk on the trailless shore a few yards between the Meadow Lane and Forest Service paths

Elevation gain: Moderate

Scenery: Beautiful; woods, streams, some exposed ridge

Exposure: Shady–90   Moderate–5   Exposed–5

Solitude: Perfect

Surface: Riding trails, logging roads, and, at Meadow Lane Lodge, small paths

Trail markings: Ritchie Trail, Ellis Trail, and Meadow Lane trails are fairly well blazed, but the interconnections between Ellis Trail and Meadow Lane trails and between Meadow Lane and Hidden Valley forest trails are short, unblazed paths.

Author's hiking time: Homestead to Meadow Lane: 5 hours; Meadow Lane to Hidden Valley Bed and Breakfast: 3 hours

Season: Open all year, but you may have to do your hiking on snow-shoes in winter

Access: Must be a guest of Homestead and Meadow Lane Lodge to hike their lands

Maps: Homestead's Ritchie Trail and Ellis Trail maps, available from the concierge; Meadow Lane Lodge trail maps available at Meadow Lane Lodge

Other uses for trail: Ritchie and Ellis trails are suitable for mountain bikes and horses

Facilities: None on trail

Shuttle: Meadow Lane and Hidden Valley innkeepers will shuttle their guests if the request is made a week in advance. Independent guide Charles Garratt (call (540) 839-3327) will provide guide and shuttle service.

Lodging info:

The Homestead, Hot Springs, Virginia, (540) 839-1766; (800) 838-1766; www.thehomestead.com; $$$$$–$$$$$$ per person includes two meals, tea, and use of the facilities

Meadow Lane Lodge, Warm Springs, Virginia, (540) 839-5959; www.meadowlanelodge.com; $$$$–$$$$$

Hidden Valley Bed and Breakfast, Hidden Valley Road
Warm Springs, Virginia, (540) 839-3178; $$$

> **Getting there:**
>
> From the intersection of Interstates 81 and 64 near Lexington, take Interstate 64 west to US 220 north (Exit 16) at Covington. Go north to Hot Springs, where the Homestead dominates the town.
>
> To get to Hidden Valley Bed and Breakfast, take US 220 approximately 5 miles north of Hot Springs to Warm Springs, turn left on Route 39 and go west about two miles to Virginia Route 621. Turn right on Route 621 and travel 1.5 miles to take a left on Forest Service Road 241. Soon after the road turns to gravel, you will see the mansion ahead, across the Jackson River.
>
> Meadow Lane Lodge is on Route 39 several miles past the turn-off for Hidden Valley.

footbridge over the highway and the intersection of three trails. The Ritchie Trail is marked with blue plastic arrows with a picture of a bicycle on them, but no name. The Ritchie and Deerlick Trails both turn left up the steep hill. For the best views on this excursion, make a quarter-mile side trip to Sunset Overlook on the right a few hundred yards up the hill. This is the best vantage for viewing the Homestead, laid out as pretty as a preening beauty queen directly below you. You can catch your breath on one of several benches or on a chair fashioned out of a tree stump.

Back on the Ritchie Trail, continue climbing until the trail swings right along the golf course and then turns sharply left uphill after a bench. Soon the Deerlick Trail will turn off to the right, but you will bear left and continue up Deerlick Mountain, a section of the misnamed Little Mountain (elevation 3,100 feet).

You won't hear the baying of hounds on moonlit nights anymore, but this double-track trail is part of a network of 100-year-old paths once used by Homestead guests and locals for foxhunts. If the fox could make it to the cliffs above Cowardin Run, he was safe. You'll spy this stream as you descend the mountain at Dunn's Gap.

When you reach the unpaved Dunn's Gap Road, turn left to follow it along the twisting Cowardin Run about one mile to the Ellis Trail, a National Forest Service footpath on the right. On the way there, you will pass two jeep trails on the right; the second, at seven-tenths of a mile, will intersect with the Ellis Trail in two miles and is the preferred route for ATVs and motorcycles.

While walking Dunn's Gap, look for waterfalls along the stream. Because Cowardin Run is a travertine stream (its waters contain large amounts of dissolved limestone), the waterfalls actually build up the underlying rock over time, a result of the stream depositing limestone as it flows.

The Ellis Trail is marked with an earthen barrier to deter vehicles, a small National Forest sign, but no name. Its course is marked (spottily) with red wooden arrows erected for an annual horse ride going in the opposite direction. At the top of the hill, continue straight, ignoring a trail on the left. You will descend into a gully and bear left past a small bike trail coming in on the right. You will ford two nameless rivulets and Hoover Run, more of a force to be reckoned with, although a few dozen feet upstream it can be jumped. You ascend through a hickory grove and pass a side trail coming in on the left.

Nearly three miles from Dunn's Gap, you will see Lake Bacova through the trees on your right. If you would like to detour to the former company town of Bacova, look for a path on the left shortly after a switchback. My landmark is a maple tree with a bulbous burl the size of a woodstove about 35 feet down the trail. On the quarter-mile path, before you reach the former Bacova headquarters, you will see Lake Bacova (really a pond) on your left and an abandoned mill in the field on your right. Although Bacova no longer operates an outlet store for its mailboxes and household items here, you may wish to see the art gallery in a former church or take your lunch at a picnic table beside the Bacova office building.

After retracing your steps back to the Ellis Trail, you'll travel near Bacova's open fields for about a half mile until you meet the wide, grassy jeep trail from Dunn's Gap Road, coming in on your right. Bear to the left toward Meadow Lane Lodge property along a nameless, but still red-blazed trail. Before long, you will cross Jerry Run. (This is a small stream, but if it has rained recently, the flow may be high for a few hours; water runs off the shale soil quickly. Go upstream to ford it.)

You will follow the trail for one and three-tenths miles as it weaves along switchbacks between mature oaks and pines, until you enter the 1,600-acre estate of Meadow Lane Lodge. This section is known as the old Katydid Trail and is marked by Meadow Lane posted signs. Take a left turn on a wide path that leads to the first visible house, the home of Meadow Lane employee Diane, and turn right across her driveway to join Route 687 for a short distance.

When you see a gated road, turn left, go uphill, and cross the yard of Phyllis, another Meadow Lane Lodge employee. (Don't worry; the no-trespassing signs don't apply to lodge guests.) Go to the end of Phyllis's driveway to cross Route 39 to reach Route 621, and follow this road about a half mile to a gate in the woods on the left (across from a mailbox on the right side of the road). The yellow-blazed trail behind the gate will lead you over a hill to Meadow Lane Lodge's barn and a greeting committee of guinea hens, peacocks, and red chickens. The lodge and several cottages will be on your left.

Meadow Lane Lodge is a country inn set on sprawling acreage along the Jackson River. The land, which has been in the Hirsh family for four

*Hiking guide Charles Garratt
crosses the Jackson River between
Meadow Lane Lodge and Hidden Valley.*

generations, is protected under a conservation easement to remain a preserve for mink, fox, waterfowl, and eagles.

You can choose among 14 accommodating rooms in the lodge or cottages spread around the property. The resort is sort of a petting zoo, a place where friendly sheep, peacocks, geese, chickens, and a donkey roam around looking for human company.

Day Two

Before you begin your hike, you may want to play a game of tennis, visit the farm animals, or go fly-fishing (catch and release) on the inn's two and a half miles of Jackson River frontage. The river is stocked with brown and rainbow trout; smallmouth bass, rock bass, bluegills, and pickerel are native.

Choose the orange trail, the path less traveled, which will kick up your heart rate to a level you won't experience anywhere else on this hike. Make the most of it; the steep portion is less than a quarter mile long.

The orange trail shares the early part of its course with several other trails and is unmarked, so you should start out from the barns on the wide, white-blazed trail. Climb a gentle hill, then join the red trail on the left, and, at a juncture with the yellow trail, turn left. Look for another left on the single-track orange trail. (Don't worry. Lodge manager Carter Acona has maps.)

After giving you a great view of Cobbler Mountain to the northeast, the trail stumbles down an extremely steep incline to a field full of Queen Anne's lace and lobelia beside the Jackson River. Unless the river is high, cross the bridge. (If the Jackson is high, you will hike to Hidden Valley on this side of the Jackson. See directions two paragraphs below.)

Go up the hill on a jeep trail and pass the Granary, remade into a suite of attractive rooms. Pause here for a water break at the pump and explore the mill museum in the barn and the reading room in the old slave cabin. When you are ready to continue, follow the road through the field to the spring. Usually you'll see myriad signs of wildlife, from raccoons and deer to bobcat and coyote. The inn's trout ponds are located here.

Although a yellow trail continues on the Meadow Lane Lodge property for another mile, it deteriorates in a half mile, shortly after leaving the riverside. At this point, you will have to leave the main trail and walk along the river on a narrow path created by fishermen. After several hundred feet, cross the Jackson on stepping stones just beyond the spot where a slough enters on the left. The opposite side is open and stony. Follow it upstream a few hundred yards to join a Forest Service trail going north along the field to Hidden Valley.

If the Jackson is high, you will want to stay on the side of the meadow where you first emerged from the orange trail. You will have to bushwhack a few hundred feet through a hedgerow on the right to emerge in an open field near the Forest Service campground and its trails. Bear to the left and you will find a trail along the riverside edge of the field.

The Forest Service trails leave the field to twist through a maze of ironwood, wild apple, locust, and other low, branchy trees. In about a half mile, you arrive on Forest Service Road 241. The Warwick mansion, now known as Hidden Valley Bed and Breakfast, is a quarter mile straight ahead. One look at the pillared, antebellum mansion, its rooms swathed in velvets, satins, and brocades, and you'll start feeling more like gentry, even before your soak.

The Homestead
Hot Springs, Virginia

Never mind that your hiking boots are not beamed upon in the Great Hall; the Homestead is a place to experience at least once in your life. . . for its ambiance, for its excesses, and for the pleasure of doing things in a grand way.

As a guest, you are entitled to breakfast and dinner in the Dining Room (these words are spoken in caps there; men, bring jacket and tie), Afternoon Tea (also in caps at The Homestead), the use of 100 miles of hiking trails, the fitness center, the pools, historical tours, and nightly movies in the theater.

There are little extras you can add if you have time and cash left over—learning falconry, the "sport of kings," for instance. Or you could try shooting sporting clays or horseback riding. But you should definitely take the waters that spawned the resort in 1766. The languid indoor pool is located in a four-story, spa building—a National Historic Landmark—that offers raspberry scrubs, herbal wraps, and mountain laurel body polish, as well as massages.

The 500 guest rooms and suites themselves are of course luxurious, having undergone a recent multimillion-dollar renovation. Traditional furnishings, plush patterned carpets and floral draperies reflect the Georgian architecture. Don't turn down the turn-down service, and remember to get an early start in the morning.

Meadow Lane Lodge
Warm Springs, Virginia

Meadow Lane Lodge traces its history back to the mid-1700s when King George III of England made a land grant to Charles Lewis. In 1754, a stockade-style fort was built here as protection for local settlers against French and Indian War raids. The frontier outpost, known as Fort Dinwiddie, was inspected by George Washington in 1755 and 1756, so in all probability he did sleep here, though likely not in the sole building of that era still standing—a small slave cabin.

Now Meadow Lane offers at least 14 rooms at the lodge and in cottages spread around the 1,600-acre estate. Some accommodations feature working fireplaces, private porches, or panoramic bay-window views. All have private bathrooms. The newest addition is the Granary, a circa 1890 renovated grain barn perched beside the Jackson River. The three-bedroom structure boasts imaginative architecture and equally imaginative furniture constructed from granary equipment.

Meadow Lane is a laid-back resort where families return year after year. The most popular activity is probably fly-casting for rainbow trout on the resort's two and a half miles of private shoreline along the highly-acclaimed Jackson River. A close second is creative loafing in front of a crackling fire or under a shade tree within sight of the barnyard menagerie. There's also swimming, tennis, croquet, canoeing, and hiking on the 20 miles of trails.

The main lodge, graced by two massive stone fireplaces, is the focal point for social gatherings and meals. After the kind of hearty breakfast I would expect if I were working on the farm, I headed for the trails.

Hidden Valley Bed and Breakfast
Warm Springs, Virginia

If this pillared, antebellum mansion looks familiar, you've probably seen the 1992 movie, *Sommersby*. Innkeepers Pam and Ron Stidham had negotiated for years with the U.S. Forest Service to allow them to lease and restore the abandoned, snake-infested home, and the renovation had

reached an optimistic stage of completion when the county stepped in with a proposal: Get publicity for your venture and give unemployed resort workers jobs by allowing Richard Gere, Jodie Foster, and other actors in for the filming of the Warner Brothers movie.

The production was not a dream come true for the couple, who had used their life savings to restore the 1848 mansion. "More like a nightmare," says Ron, who saw the movie crew tear out a custom-built antique closet so that a portrait could be hung and use earth-moving equipment on an archaeological site. On the first day, Pam told actor Richard Gere that he was never to skid his Lexus into her driveway again. "He treated us with respect after that," Ron says. "He even introduced us to his mom and dad."

Despite the layered, beaded curtains, covetable antiques, and heirloom knickknacks, the Stidhams maintain an air of informality. The front door stands open on cool evenings, and children over six are welcome in any of the three guest rooms, an anomaly in fine bed-and-breakfast circles.

Three benign female ghosts have been reported in the house, although the Stidhams have never seen them. Surrounded by almost 9,000 acres of U.S. Forest land, you're likely to sleep soundly from the moment your head hits the pillow until you hear Pam's footsteps bringing a doily-covered beverage to your door in the morning. The sustaining breakfasts include enough sweet breads to tuck away for a later snack should you decide to explore Hidden Valley's miles of beautiful trails or fish on the Jackson River. The Stidhams keep several beater bicycles to lend. A morning of mountain fog, flowers dazzling with dew, and the omnipresent deer is not to be missed.

The Stidhams will shuttle guests to their cars at Hot Springs or Meadow Lane Lodge if the guests make that request with their reservation.

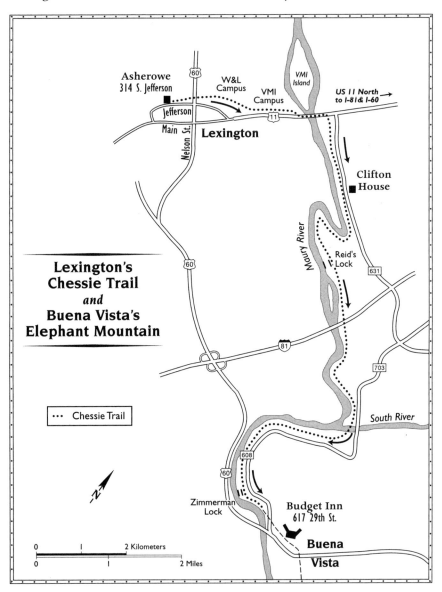

Getting there:

To get to Asherowe in Lexington, take Exit 188B (US 60N) off Interstate 81 and go northwest through town to Jefferson Street. Turn left on Jefferson and go three blocks.

To get to the Budget Inn in downtown Buena Vista, take 188A (US 60E) off Interstate 81 and go east for 5 miles. Budget Inn is on the left.

Lexington's Chessie Trail and Buena Vista's Elephant Mountain

This hike represents two extremes: a civilized ramble on the wide Chessie Trail along riverside and pasture, then an energetic climb up Elephant Mountain on a narrow trail used more by wildlife than humans.

The Lowdown

This walk stretches from Lexington's historical district to Buena Vista's mountain wilderness. The Chessie Trail, maintained by Virginia Military Institute, starts at VMI Island, but your trek begins at the doorstep of Asherowe and meanders past the historic sites of downtown Lexington and the Washington & Lee University and Virginia Military Institute campuses.

Lexington's charming brick streets, restored 19th-century shops, and Civil War history make it an excellent walking tour. In fact, town carriage and ghost tours capitalize on all the stories that have taken place in Lexington's buildings. You can pick up a map at the visitors' center at 106 East Washington Street. Must-sees include Stonewall Jackson's house at 8 East Washington Street, where the life of the eccentric Confederate general is interpreted daily, and the Lee Chapel on the William & Lee campus. On the adjacent VMI campus, just down Letcher Avenue, you can visit the George Marshall Museum and the VMI Museum, with its stuffed hide of Stonewall Jackson's horse, Little Sorrell.

From Asherowe, head northeast on Jefferson Street, moving downhill, until it intersects with US 11. Continue on to the Maury River, where the Chessie Trail begins at a picnic area on VMI Island behind VMI. At this spot, you can see the stone abutments where the Great Valley Road crossed the Maury River. After the Kanawha Canal reached

Key at-a-Glance Information

Length: Lexington to Buena Vista: 8.7 miles; Buena Vista loop over Elephant Mountain: 7.3 miles

Difficulty: Chessie Trail to Buena Vista is easy; Buena Vista trails up Elephant Mountain are moderate to strenuous.

Elevation gain: Negligible on Chessie; more than 600 feet on Elephant Mountain

Scenery: Woods and pasture with cliffs and river views on Chessie; deep forest with sweeping views on Elephant Mountain

Exposure: Shady–70   Moderate–10   Exposed–20

Solitude: Lexington side of Chessie sees moderate traffic; perfect on Elephant Mountain

Surface: Hard-packed dirt

Trail markings: Chessie is well marked and obvious; Elephant Mountain trails are small paths that are not well marked at Buena Vista trailheads

Author's hiking time: Lexington to Buena Vista: 5.5 hours (including some sightseeing in Lexington); Elephant Mountain loop: 4 hours

Season: Year-round, although hikers should avoid Elephant Mountain during peak hunting season in November; Elephant Mountain trails may be impassable in winter.

Access: No permits or fees

Maps: Chessie Nature Trail at Lexington Visitors' Center, U.S. Geological Survey map of Buena Vista; U.S. Forest Service map 509

Other uses for trail: Chessie is okay for cross-country skiing, but biking is not appropriate on either trail.

Facilities: None on trail

Shuttle: Asherowe bed-and-breakfast and Budget Inn will shuttle guests who make prior arrangements.

Lodging info:

Asherowe, 314 South Jefferson Street Lexington, Virginia (540) 463-4219; $

Budget Inn, 617 West 29th Street, Buena Vista, Virginia; (540) 261-2156; $

Alternative lodging:

In Lexington, the visitors' center has a list of bed-and-breakfasts and motels within the town. In Buena Vista, the Buena Vista Motel (call (800) 286-6965) is two miles from the end of the Chessie Trail.

Reid's Lock is one of several locks still visible
on the Maury River along the Chessie Trail.

Lexington from Richmond in 1860, the island was lined with wharves and warehouses. Now it's a grassy park.

You'll find no bathrooms on the Chessie, but benches are spaced about a mile apart for the first five miles from VMI Island.

The footbridge from VMI Island was not repaired after a flood in the 1990s, so pedestrians take the US 11 bridge over the Maury and turn right on a lane running parallel to the Old Buena Vista Road (Route 631). Don't be discouraged by the 18-wheelers parked in this alley. Within a block, the trail begins to look more like an English lane than an industrial back lot.

The first indication you are on the right trail is a concrete post on the right bearing the inscription "BF-19." In the days when the Richmond and Allegheny Railroad ran here, this sign let the train engineer know that he was 19 miles from Balcony Falls, where the Maury joins the James. Signs for BF-16, BF-14, and BF-12 still stand along the trail.

As you make your way down this alley, you'll see increasing evidence that you are indeed on the two-lane Chessie Trail—a footbridge in the distance and a sign. The large, brick house across the road on the left is Clifton, the 1815 home of Major John Alexander, who also built the Alexander-Withrow building in Lexington. Robert E. Lee used to watch boat races on the Maury from the lawn of Clifton. As president of Washington College (now Washington & Lee), Lee instituted rowing as a team sport.

Just beyond Clifton is the rock-lined Wye, a short section of track shaped like an inverted **Y** to enable trains to back up, change directions, and back into the station in town. As the train came into Lexington, it often lost steam on the grade behind VMI. Cadets at the military institute sometimes greased the tracks to make it difficult for trains carrying the weekend dates of W&L boys to reach the station. The cadets would courteously help their rivals' dates from the halted train and escort them into town.

Most local people access the trail just west of the Wye, where the Chessie enters a pretty wooded area along the river. For the next three miles, the trail runs under a canopy of ash, sycamore, and box elder, often through gated areas where horses and cattle graze. High cliffs on the north side are hung with columbine, coral bells, and poison ivy, which turns a glorious red in fall. You will occasionally see shallow caves on the left side of the trail. The limestone here ranges from the Middle Cambrian to Middle Ordovician periods (550 to 450 million years ago).

The 1860 canal system used the river most of the way from Lexington to Buena Vista. Two miles downstream from VMI Island you can see Reid's Lock and Dam, where boats were held so that the horses and mules that pulled the vessel on the towpath could be ferried across the stream to a towpath on the other side. The wide stone shelf here is a popular picnic spot.

Three miles out, Interstate 81 passes high overhead, its traffic heard but not seen by pedestrians below. Shortly after this, you'll see 160-foot cliffs rising from the south side of the river. Their folds were created when the Appalachian Mountains were formed.

As you walk between fenced grazing areas along the way, you will have to remove your daypack to pass through a narrow gap at the edge of each gate. The cattle seldom show much interest in hikers and may continue lying on the trail as you pass.

If you look across the Maury about four miles out, you will see South River Lock. This is a point between Lexington and Buena Vista where canal boats left the river completely and traveled a canal that allowed them to bypass the confluence of the North (now Maury) and South Rivers. The two-step lock is partially filled in, but parts of the rock walls can still be seen. Soon after this, the Chessie Trail crosses South River on a 235-foot footbridge; the water is often clear enough to reveal trout swimming over the gravel.

Continue a short distance to another access point, the end of an old county road. In a nearby pasture, you can see a concrete whistle post. The "W" on the top of the four-foot post reminded the engineer to blow his whistle (long, long, short, and long) upon approaching the old road. In the summer the pastures are full of flowers—soapwort, phlox, black-eyed Susans, chicory, and thistles.

At six miles, you may be able to see the Ben Salem Lock on the other side of the river. A cliff on the north is veined with calcite and quartz. Zimmerman's Lock, this time on the close side of the river, is reportedly a good fishing spot for bass.

The Chessie Trail ends on Route 608, just before the US 60 bridge into Buena Vista. The half-mile walk beside US 60, past a factory and into Buena Vista, is not especially scenic, but lodging is clean, adequate, and cheap. Both of the town's two motels have restaurants adjacent.

Day Two

Your second day of hiking will make a loop of city streets and wooded trails as you walk through and above the village of Buena Vista. If you would prefer a shorter hike, get the Budget Inn owner to drop you off at a parking area two and eight-tenths miles out of town on US 60 before it reaches the Blue Ridge Parkway. From there, the hike back to the hotel is about four miles over the mountain using Indian Gap Trail and hiking through Laurel Park, or just over five and a half miles using the Reservoir Hollow Trail.

Take 13th Street from Magnolia ten blocks to Pine, turn right, and take a path from the end of 12th Street into the woods. You will pass the police shooting range on the left soon after entering the forest. In early 2000, there was no sign naming the trail, but the path is obvious as you follow a small stream up the gap. The forest is mostly hardwoods—dogwood, nuts, and hawthorn—in the lower areas, with more blueberry bushes, oaks, and dying scrub pine as you ascend.

After about a half mile, you come to a fork. Veer up the mountain to the left instead of following the right-hand path to the foundation of the old reservoir.

Watch out for snakes seeking the stream's moisture in summer. The trail is lined with rocks. Because so few people use this trail, we took along a spider wand, a stick we swung in front of us as we walked to remove cobwebs and frighten off pests.

Elephant Mountain looms behind Buena Vista.

You can hear the flutelike song of the wood thrush as you gain altitude and distance from town. The first birdcalls you'll hear are likely to be juncos, flycatchers, and pileated woodpeckers.

It takes some imagination and distance to see the mountain you are climbing as a sleeping elephant. Perhaps the best perspective is from back in town on the opposite side of the Maury, up at Inspiration Point lookout in Maury Park. From the trail, it feels as though you are climbing a very long elephant trunk. Reached on an out-and-back side trail, the Elephant is 2,101 feet at its peak. The Elephant Mountain Trail, which is one and two-tenths miles one way, is an optional detour on this hike. It departs two miles from the start of Reservoir Hollow Trail, and it is small, steep, unmarked, and almost overgrown by blueberries in spots. At its ridgetop terminus, this trail will give you a great view of Buena Vista. Be aware that it is an out-and-back hike, so don't be tricked into following those small deer paths that radiate out from the peak—or you'll end up bushwhacking over rocky rattlesnake habitat, as we did.

Rattlers. We expected to see one striking at us with every stumbling step we took down the old rockslides on the face of Elephant Mountain. We had heard that area was once prime rattlesnake hunting territory. We half longed for an encounter, so that we could realize our worst fears and be done with them, but it was not to be.

Our anxiety was more a product of our own imagination than reality. In fact, timber rattlers are considered shy and choose flight over fight if possible. They will try to warn and escape before they strike. Of the 8,000 people who are bitten by venomous snakes each year in this country, 70 to 80 percent were in the process of harassing the snake. Only 9 to 15 percent of those bitten die.

Besides, rattlers are not what you would call prolific. In the Appalachians, females might take as long as nine years to mature and they only breed every two to four years. When they do reproduce, the majority of their babies are killed by hawks, owls, foxes, coyote, and raccoons. Timber rattlesnakes are declining precipitously in this country, so much so that they have become a protected species in Virginia. So it's unlikely that you will see one, and if you do, stomping on the ground will probably send it on its way. Statistically, bees pose more of a threat to your life.

Still, I'd recommend hiking boots on this hike.

Return to the Reservoir Hollow Trail and follow it until it joins the Indian Gap Trail six-tenths of a mile past the juncture with Elephant Mountain Trail. Turn left, descending through second-growth hardwoods along Indian Gap Run. You will pass pink lady's slippers, wood betony, blackberries, and black raspberries along the creek. The trail is usually maintained, but the creek has washed away a few feet of the trail in a few places. The path ends in a community ballpark and small playground named "Bubba's Backyard," in honor of a former coach. The whole development is called Laurel Park, and its access road will take you out on 21st Street. Follow the street down about eight blocks to Highway 501/Magnolia Avenue, turn right and head toward US 60 and the motel. You will pass the 1891 General Store, a great place to stop for ice cream and experience a working store museum.

Asherowe
Lexington, Virginia

The Asherowe exudes comfortable charm. The antique dressers, canopy bed, and doilies make for an attractive room, but the place is not so dense with antique knickknacks that a hiker fears the consequences of turning around wearing a daypack.

Hostess Yvonne Emerson is herself comfortable and flexible with breakfast times, arrival times, and checkout times. With a little prior notice, she is happy to shuttle hikers. And if you'd like to practice your French or German, the high-school and university language instructor is game. She loves to converse about photography, books, and cats, including her two resident ladies, Calypso and Aude.

Guests are invited to make themselves comfortable in the library, the living room, on the porch, or in the garden area of this gaily painted mustard and red house in Lexington's historic district. The home is four blocks from the Lee Chapel and five from the Marshall Museum and the Stonewall Jackson House. Lexington's ghost tour passes within a block of the Asherowe to wind up at Stonewall Jackson Cemetery. You can make the two-block trip on your own; the Civil War hero's grave is often adorned with Jackson's favorite pre-battle snack—lemons.

Breakfast in Asherowe's dining room is a several course affair, often ending with a sweet pastry and fruit.

Budget Inn
Buena Vista, Virginia

The Budget Inn, located a half mile from the end of the Chessie Trail, doesn't pretend to be anything other than a simple, efficient motel. No bed-and-breakfasts exist in Buena Vista to serve the George Washington National Forest trails, but for years, the Budget Inn has accommodated Appalachian Trail hikers with low rates, a laundry, and a sandwich shop on the premises. You can walk to Buena Vista's Reservoir Hollow and Indian Gap Trails from the motel.

The 42 rooms have been newly renovated and offer remote control television with HBO and free local phone calls. There's also a microwave and refrigerator available to guests. You can see the elephant-shaped mountain that looms up behind Buena Vista from some of the motel's windows.

For entertainment, you may want to stroll around the grounds of the nearby Southern Virginia College, whose administrative offices are housed in a former resort hotel, or walk over to the 1891 General Store for a sweet treat. The General Store is a combination mercantile museum and working store with brass cash registers, a potbellied stove, and a variety of goods. Both the store and the college are within a six-block stroll.

The Budget Inn manager, a transplant from India, is happy to accommodate hiker guests. He'll give advice or even shuttle you back to your car if you give him some notice. He's a nice guy. What more can you say about a man who has adopted a three-legged dog and made it the motel mascot?

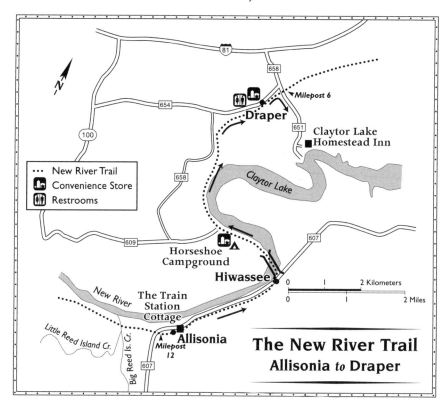

The New River Trail
Allisonia to Draper

Getting there:

For road access to Allisonia, take Exit 94 off Interstate 81 and take old Route 100 to Route 672 (Lowman's Ferry Road), where you will turn right, eventually crossing Claytor Lake. Then turn right again on Route 693 to cross over Little Irish Mountain and pass Hiwassee to Allisonia. You will see the train depot on your left, just past the Pentecostal Holiness church.

To get to Claytor Lake Homestead Inn, take the Draper exit off Interstate 81 and follow Route 658 east through town. When 658 turns right, continue across the trail on Route 651 and over a hill. The driveway is on your left.

The New River Trail

Allisonia to Draper

Walk beside the northern hemisphere's oldest river on an abandoned railbed. After starting at a former iron-mining town, this path travels through forest, beside Claytor Lake, over trestles, and by flowering pastureland.

The Lowdown

The New River Trail follows the oldest river in the northern hemisphere. When the Blue Ridge Mountains were thrust upward by inner earth movements, the New River was cutting down on the raw rock. The New is one of the few rivers that has maintained its ancient northern course, as it flows up through West Virginia to join with the Kanawha and the Ohio Rivers.

How you do this hike depends upon the part of your body you want to strengthen. You can start at Allisonia and give your calves a workout on the gradual uphill grade, or you can start at Draper and carry your dinner and breakfast, putting the stress on your upper body. The Allisonia Train Station is charming, but unless you work something out with owners Don and Chipper Holt, you'll have to pack in your meals. Allisonia has no restaurant and, at this point, no store, except for the soda and snack machines outside the Holt's gun shop.

So, your trek will be less complicated if you begin at Allisonia and spend your first night in the Train Station listening to the riffles of the New River just before it hits the sluggish backwater of Claytor Lake. If you're especially imaginative, you may also hear a train whistle—the Cripple Creek branch of the Norfolk and Western Railway clanged past within feet of your sleeping quarters—or the angry shouts that led to a

Key at-a-Glance Information

Length: 7.5 miles

Difficulty: Fairly easy 1 to 2 percent grade

Elevation gain: About 200 feet

Scenery: Pasture, woods, and views of lake

Exposure: Shady–50   Moderate–15   Exposed–35

Solitude: Moderate use on weekends

Surface: Cinder and packed dirt

Trail markings: Only at crossings, but trail is obvious

Author's hiking time: 3 hours

Season: Year-round

Access: No permits or fees

Maps: New River Trail Park map, available from New River Trail State Park, Box 126 F, Foster Falls, Virginia 24360; (540) 699-6778

Other uses for trail: Mountain biking, cross-country skiing, horseback riding

Facilities: Toilets and snacks at Draper and Allisonia; bathrooms, pool, and snacks at Horseshoe Campground off trail near milepost 9.5

Shuttle: Tangent Outfitters (call (540) 674-5202). They also rent bikes, canoes, and arrange fishing and riding packages.

Innkeepers at Train Station and Claytor Lake Homestead Inn often can shuttle guests who make advance reservations.

Lodging info:

Claytor Lake Homestead Inn, Draper, Virginia
(540) 980-6777 or (800) 676-LAKE; $$$$$

The Train Station, 1530 Julia Simpkins Road, Allisonia, Virginia
(540) 980-2051; $–$$

shooting in front of the station many decades ago. All I can guarantee, though, is the river.

Before you plunge into your walk and leave Allisonia, you can accept the Holt's invitation to try out their pontoon boat on this lazy section of river-turning-into-lake, stretch your legs on a short warm-up hike south to roust the vultures roosting in the white cliffs, or look around at the turn-of-the-century architecture. Although train service began here in 1885, Allisonia didn't really become a boomtown for another decade. The gingerbread and Queen Anne homes represent scant remnants of a town that boasted four general stores, two schools, three mills, and two hotels. The Holts, who moved from Charlotte, North Carolina, in 1992, have had their hands in the restoration of many of the buildings you see.

The railroad into Allisonia was built in the early 1880s by Norfolk and Western Railway officials who believed that Wythe County held the largest, most diverse supply of metals and minerals in the nation. The railroad hauled out loads of lead, iron, and zinc. Although at least five iron mines were built near Allisonia, their lives were relatively short; in 1915 state and federal laws were passed banning the dumping of muddy wastewater from the ore-washing operations into the New River, and the mines closed within two years.

The only evidence of mineral wealth you will see in this section is the private road to a strip mine operated by the Hoover Color Corporation. The iron-oxide ores mined here are used as pigment for paint, so the

The New River widens into Claytor Lake north of Allisonia.

area, about a mile northeast of Allisonia, is referred to as "paint rocks" or "paint banks." The strip mine is located near milepost 11.5 and the plant near milepost 10.4.

After you leave Allisonia, walking northeast on the trail, you will see the New River on your left. Near Norfolk and Western milepost 12 (the few N&W posts that remain lag behind freshly painted park mileposts as they count southward), you can see a boat ramp provided by the Appalachian Power Company's Claytor Lake Dam Project and the Virginia Wildlife Commission. At least 50 vehicles can park here.

At milepost 10.2, you cross one of only three bridges on the entire trail that span the New River. The 951-foot Hiwassee Trestle was built in 1931, the year the Claytor Lake Dam was completed. You enter the forest under a green arbor of ash, locust, and maple. The trail begins a steady two-percent uphill grade that at first lulls you with its ease, but within a few miles, your muscles are aware of the exertion. The ascent continues until it reaches "the Hump" a mile past Draper.

About a half mile after milepost 10—just before the Delton Branch trestle in Dog Bite Hollow—a small side trail on the left leads up about 100 feet to the Horseshoe Campground and its seasonal store. This is a good time to take a juice break, go for a swim in the park pool ($2 a day for hikers), or watch campground manager Karita Knisely build her willow twig furniture. In 2000, Knisely added a new line—chairs and tables crafted from New River driftwood.

A former New River Trail State Park ranger, Knisely holds a wealth of knowledge about the natural and human history of the trail. She has her own history as well, having fought a successful battle to stop the trails from being surfaced with noxious ash from local power plants. "I believe the squeaky wheel can make a difference," she says.

Continuing on the main trail, you pass a few houses, some cliffs, and earn some impressive views of the lake. The concrete piers that supported a train-engine water tank are all that is left of the railroad town of Delton. The town disappeared under the water when the New River was dammed to form Claytor Lake. Near milepost 8, you cross the 420-foot Davidson Trestle over a small tributary. By now, you have left the lake behind and are beginning to climb into the forest and pasture above its shores.

You will eventually pass over two other long trestles over small streams and emerge in rolling farmland. Crabapple trees and blackberry bushes border the trail. To reduce its climbing grade, the railroad bed cuts into the earth. The steep banks are now hung with ferns, moss, columbines, and assorted wildflowers. At about milepost 6, a horizontal cable with vertical extensions hangs over the track. Once it warned people walking on top of the railway cars that an overhead bridge was coming up. The wooden bridge is now gone, but you may be able to spot a piece of the concrete foundation on the bank above the tracks.

Trestles of the New River Trail vault pastures near Draper.

A quarter mile after crossing the Loan Branch bridge, you come to the village of Draper. Although the station is gone, a covered picnic area, a trail map sign, a parking lot, and a restroom have taken its place along the railbed. Across Route 658 is Bryson's Grocery, which serves limited breakfasts, sandwiches, ice cream, snacks, and cold drinks.

To reach Claytor Lake Homestead Inn, pass the parking lot and turn left off the trail on Route 651. You will follow this lake-access road over the hill one and two-tenths miles until you spot the driveway for the inn on the left.

Claytor Lake Homestead Inn
Draper, Virginia

When you turn into the driveway of this lakeside inn, keep your eyes focused on the view just beyond—the majestic cliffs and azure lake. The inn's stone wraparound porch and all but one of its six bedrooms have stunning views of Claytor Lake as it curves around the jutting point where the inn is perched. The view is so renewing that many guests choose to dine on the front terrace or at the screened cabana on the beach.

Claytor Lake Homestead Inn owns 550 feet of frontage for swimming, boating, fishing, or sunning. Along with your room and a gourmet

breakfast, guest privileges include complimentary use of inn rowboats at a spot that one professional guide has declared the best fishing on the lake.

The rambling farmhouse is attractively comfortable with a glassed-in porch dedicated to bird-watching. Guests have spotted scarlet tanagers, purple finches, indigo buntings, bluebirds, cedar waxwings, and many other species flitting in the bushes or feeding at the house bird feeders. The room is also an excellent private nook to exchange stories and watch the sunrise.

The living rooms are decorated with antiques, near-antiques, and overstuffed furniture that invites lolling. You can rock in an assortment of rocking chairs, each with a Pulaski County past. An old enamel wood-burning stove stands at the entrance to the modern kitchen.

The three-course breakfasts always begin with fruit and end with something sweet—honey poundcake with fruit is a perpetual favorite. The middle course includes bread, sautéed potatoes, and a meat or egg dish—frittata, crab quiche with a whole wheat crust, pork tenderloins with chutney, or country ham and redeye gravy. "We try to give guests a breakfast that makes them think of skipping lunch," says owner Diane Whitehead. The inn will also prepare bag lunches upon request. If you wish dinner, you should make the request with your reservation.

The inn offers five bedrooms upstairs plus a downstairs suite with a private bar, and it has plans for renovating a honeymoon cottage on the grounds. Private and shared baths are available.

The Train Station at Allisonia
Allisonia, Virginia

Don and Chipper Holt bought the Allisonia train depot to use for a woodworking shop, but soon realized they couldn't resist restoring it to its 1885 look. Now Train Station guests sleep in the restored waiting room, breakfast in the telegraph office, and bathe just behind the ticket window. Though they no longer hear the whistle of the Norfolk and Western, they will likely see walkers, bikers, and equestrians enjoying the 57-mile New River Trail as it passes their door.

The three-room apartment is cozily furnished with a hodgepodge of beautiful and campy collectibles that Chipper refers to as "antique junk."

A roughly ridden rocking horse looks down from atop the closet over a bedroom decorated with quilts, railroad memorabilia, and knickknacks from the turn of the century. The living room, whose couch folds out into another bed, is dominated by a slew of woven baskets suspended from an ancient ladder on the ceiling.

A primitive pine chest rescued from a neighbor's yard serves as a coffee table, nestled against a dainty spool rocker and a towering jelly cabinet.

The telegraph operator's office looks oddly appropriate as a kitchen, with its green and white cabinets and a sink sunk into the counter. If you look closely at the curtains, you'll note that they are hung from railroad spikes. The teakettle, which could easily date from the 1940s, has been transformed into country art by an array of hand-painted wildflowers.

Perhaps the single classiest feature of the restored depot is the custom molding Don Holt created in the shop in the back of the building. Deep forest green molding in all the rooms coordinates with the exterior trim.

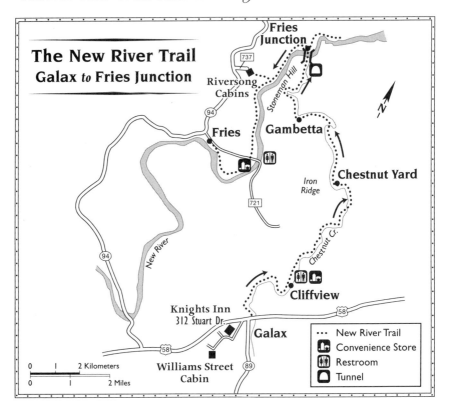

Getting there:

To get to Galax lodging, take Exit 14 off Interstate 77 to US 58 west. When you reach Galax, turn left onto West Stuart Drive off US 58, about three-tenths of a mile past the park entrance at Chestnut Creek. The Knights Inn will be up a steep hill on your right. For Williams Street Cabin, continue on the mostly residential West Stuart six more blocks, make a 90-degree right turn with it and look for Alderman Street. Turn left on Alderman, go down a dip, and start up a hill. Look for Williams Street on your right. The cabin will be obvious on the right among the contemporary houses as you crest the hill.

Fries is accessed by taking US 58 west of Galax to Route 94 and going 9 miles north. To find Riversong cabins, turn off Route 94 onto Route 737 and go nine-tenths of a mile to Riversong Road.

The New River Trail

Galax to Fries Junction

Hike along one of the prettiest, wildest sections of Virginia's longest and skinniest state park. The trail, built on the former Norfolk and Western railroad bed, twists along a creek, through a tunnel, past cliffs, and crosses over the New River.

The Lowdown

The 59-mile New River Trail's most southern terminus is in Galax, a mill town named after a wild plant residents once collected for florists. The trail begins at the US 58 bridge across Chestnut Creek; you can walk there easily along the quiet streets by retracing the driving directions to your hotel or cabin. If you slept at the Williams Street Cabins, retrace the way you drove in by walking down the hill to Alderman Street. Turn left and continue down the hill, then up as you approach West Stuart Drive. Turn right, and in six blocks you will pass the Knights Inn. Continue following West Stuart a block until it reaches US 58, turn right, and in three-tenths of a mile you will reach the entrance to the converted railway that is now the New River Trail. The original railroad extended into the factory district upstream from the trail parking area.

As you start on the double-track path, you will see that maples, ash, and other hardwoods line the trail now. In the New River Line's heyday, it was bordered by stockyards for the first quarter mile, up to current milepost 51.

Two miles up the trail, at the intersection with Route 721, is the little community of Cliffview, dominated by the Cliffside Mansion, former home of Baldwin-Felts Detective Agency owner Thomas Lee Felts. This company supplied guards to the coal companies of central Appalachia and Colorado during the violent labor struggles of the first part of this

Key at-a-Glance Information

Length: Galax to Riversong Cabins: 12.5 miles; additional loop to Fries: add 8.5 miles

Difficulty: Easy 1 to 2 percent grade

Elevation gain: Negligible

Scenery: Beautiful; mostly wooded with cliffs and river views

Exposure: Shady–80   Moderate–10   Exposed–10

Solitude: Fairly quiet, except near Galax on weekends

Surface: Hard packed dirt, some gravel

Trail markings: Only at crossings, but trail is obvious

Author's hiking time: 4 hours

Season: Year-round

Access: No permits or fees

Maps: New River Trail Park map, available at Cliffview Visitors' Center

Other uses for trail: Mountain biking, cross-country skiing, horseback riding

Facilities: Snacks, water, and bathroom at Cliffview; food at Galax and Fries

Shuttle: Jim Alley will shuttle Riversong guests back to their cars if they make this arrangement with their cabin reservation. Otherwise, use shuttle by Tangent Outfitters (call (540) 674-5202). Tangent also rents bikes and canoes and arranges fishing and riding packages.

Lodging info:

Williams Street Cabin, Williams Street, Galax, Virginia; (540) 236-3172; $–$$ (meals extra)

Knights Inn, 312 Stuart Drive , Galax, Virginia; (540) 236-5117 or (800) 843-5644; $

Riversong Cabins, 916 Swinney Hollow Road
Fries, Virginia; (877) 748-3775; www.riversongcabins.com
$$$ for whole cabin (no meals provided)

Alternative lodging:

In Galax, there is the Galax Motel (call (540) 236-9935) and Super 8 (call (540) 236-5127).

*Water ripples north over a rocky
bed at the Shoals of the New.*

century. The John Sayles movie, *Matewan*, dramatizes a conflict between Baldwin-Felts detectives and members of the United Mine Workers of America in southern West Virginia. Seven Baldwin-Felts detectives were killed in that 1920 gun battle, including Felts' two brothers and another man from Galax. They are buried in Felts Memorial Cemetery near the trail on Glendale Street in Galax.

Prior to Felts's ownership of the farm, Sidney Blair owned and operated Blair Forge here. Iron ore came from mines downstream on Chestnut Creek.

A ranger station located beside the trail at Cliffview has maps, running water, and a public restroom. The Cliffview Trading Post across Route 721 sells snacks and rents bicycles April through November.

Continue from Cliffview into a forest of white pine, filberts, hickory, and wild roses. Extensive underground and pit mining for iron occurred on the ridges to the west of the trail near milepost 47. You can see the grading for the railroad siding to the mines on the left. A small stream that enters Chestnut Creek through a stone culvert still picks up such a high acidity level flowing through the mining watershed that most of the surrounding trees and plants have been killed. Chestnut Creek's aquatic life appears to have adapted to the high acidity levels because fish are still swimming around downstream from the polluted stream.

You can relax on a bench and admire Chestnut Creek's waterfalls at milepost 46. Ahead are banks of rhododendrons and a jeep trail that was probably the railroad siding for the first iron mine on the creek. Nothing remains of the inn and store that once stood here. In another mile (milepost 45), you'll see an old ore loading dock, discolored from the rusty iron. The Iron Ridge Mine operated here. The Chestnut Yard railroad turntable located near here positioned engines in the proper direction. A wide flat area and bits of concrete are all that remain.

Cross over another trestle and arrive in two miles at Gambetta Crossing, marked by a church. Here Virginia 602 provides public access to the trail.

The Chestnut Creek Tunnel, near milepost 40, cuts through 193 feet of rock, making it the longer of two tunnels on the New River Trail. Watch out for poison ivy crowding the trail. Just after the tunnel, the trail crosses its longest trestle (1,059 feet long) over the New River at Fries Junction, to join the Fries prong of the New River Trail.

The New River provides the only habitat in the whole state for the Carolina silver bell tree. In late April, you can spot their distinctive white flowers. The silver bell attract a number of insect pests, which in turn attract the Mexican warbler—a bird you won't hear in many other Virginia localities.

To reach Riversong Cabins, turn toward Fries and continue walking on the trail just over a mile, past the Lower Shoals of Double Shoals to milepost 41.

About 50 yards upstream from the milepost, a path leads uphill to the cabins. This trail is about 250 yards long and is marked with yellow posts.

For those folks who still have a good head of steam (or who want to continue walking the following day), the trail to Fries beckons. It is almost four miles one way, or just over eight miles out-and-back if you return to Riversong Cabins.

Continue past the Riversong Cabins beside the New, where it rolls over rapids for almost two miles. Shawn Hash, owner of Tangent Outfitters, says this section of the New has provided such great fishing that he's glad it's relatively inaccessible. The steep banks are gardens for loosestrife, blazing star, tick trefoil, flowering spurge, and woodland sunflower. Along the water, you can often see kingfishers, crows, and osprey.

A little past milepost 43, you come to Low Water Bridge, so named because the bridge is lower that the average flood level of the river. Once

Dixon's ferry operated here; now a convenience store dispenses snacks, necessities, and the news. A telephone and picnic tables make this a good place to relax and admire the limestone cliffs across the river.

As you continue another mile and a half toward Fries, the landscape opens up to meadow, where you see musk mallow, butterfly weed, iron-weed, Virginia dayflower, spiderwort, and cardinal flower. The town of Fries (population 800) is located on the north bank of the New River. Fries was developed as a cotton-mill company town by Colonel F. H. Fries, but the mill has closed and most of the residents are retirees. Above the New River Trail State Park sign on the hill is the recreation center with bowling, swimming, and other facilities. The stores and restaurant are straight ahead.

Williams Street Cabin
Galax, Virginia

There is only one Williams Street Cabin, a truly unique log-and-chink cabin hauled in from the fields of Surry County, North Carolina. And because there is only one and because it is often occupied, this book also lists a chain motel as substitute lodging. But the lovingly reconstructed Williams Street Cabin and its charming folk-art furnishings are well worth the modest rental price, if owner Mary Guyunn tells you the cabin is available.

The wooden front porch is a nice enough place to relax, but the private back porch overlooking bird feeders and a wooded area is even more enticing. Inside, a quilt-covered double bed stretches out toward the fireplace. The original chestnut beams, hand-built doors, and small rooms give it a cozy feel.

The romance is downstairs; upstairs is the pajama party, with three large beds and two trundle beds, all attractively covered with quilts and handmade throws. The bathroom addition is thoroughly modern but crafted with lots of exposed wood and plaster for an old look.

Restaurants are about five blocks away on Oldtown and Main Streets, and the trail is a mile northeast.

Knights Inn
Galax, Virginia

It's now the Knights Inn, part of a chain, but this landmark motel that takes up a whole hillside in west Galax was once known as the Roselane. The huge floral pattern of its lobby carpet, the crisp white rockers lined up under its awnings, and the sprawling one-story lodge units give away the building's origin as one of the early motels of the interstate era.

The inn's 49 newly-redecorated rooms are pleasant, with room to move around between the light, bright furnishings. The floral theme set in the lobby persists in each room. Housekeeping here is scrupulous.

The Knights Inn features a free continental breakfast of donuts and coffee, free local calls, and free HBO. The outdoor pool is open May through September. The motel is located within a short walk of Galax's downtown restaurants and just off US 58, a half mile from the trailhead on Chestnut Creek.

Riversong Cabins
Fries, Virginia

These cabins—they're really little houses—are the brainchildren of Jim Alley, who moved back to Fries after selling insurance in Charlotte for 27 years. He built six Riversong cabins on a steep, wooded hillside above the trail. On any night, the view of the Shoals from the barbecue deck and the west cottage is impressive. Each cabin has two bedrooms, a gas log fireplace, a fully equipped kitchen, and a satellite dish on the porch. All the comforts of home, but few of the distractions.

If it came down to choosing among the 50 channels on the television and the old-fashioned swing on the porch, I'd choose the swing; the river does have a song as it ripples over the Shoals of the New, and I'd want to hear it late into the evening.

Jim Alley has heard the ultimate river song. When ice breaks up in February, the New becomes a cracking, pouring torrent over the rapids. A steady diet of percussion would be wearing perhaps, but for one night it's fiercely exciting.

For dinner, you will need to pack in provisions or walk two extra miles down the trail toward Fries to the convenience store on Low Water Bridge. If you're feeling very frisky, you may even want to go all the way in to Fries to the nameless restaurant that serves meatloaf, steak fries, and vanilla pudding for $3.50. There's also a pizza place.

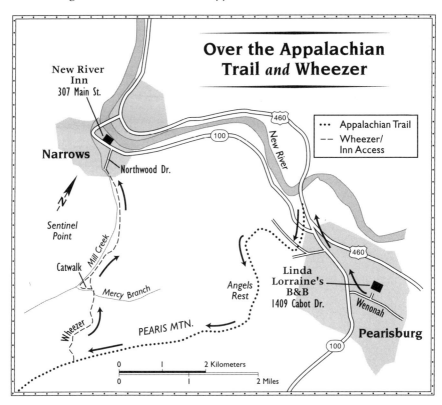

Over the Appalachian Trail *and* Wheezer

New River Inn
307 Main St.

Narrows

Northwood Dr.

··· Appalachian Trail
— — Wheezer/
    Inn Access

New River

460

100

Sentinel Point

Catwalk

Mill Creek

Mercy Branch

Wheezer

PEARIS MTN.

Angels Rest

Linda Lorraine's B&B
1409 Cabot Dr.

460

Wenonah

Pearisburg

100

N

0   1   2 Kilometers

0   1   2 Miles

Getting there:

To reach Linda Lorraine's, take the Pearisburg/Ripplemead exit off US 460. and follow US 460 Business (Wenonah Street) toward Pearisburg. After entering Pearisburg, take a right on Horsley Drive. As you crest the hill, you'll see Linda Lorraine's directly before you. Veer right to the driveway.

For the New River Inn, take US 460 to the Narrows exit and follow Route 61 over the bridge to downtown Narrows, where you will turn left on Route 100, the main street. The inn is on the left, just after the post office.

Pearisburg to Narrows over the Appalachian Trail and Wheezer

The Appalachian Trail up Pearis Mountain to Angel's Rest is legendary for its rigor and its view. But that 1,650-foot gain is just the first one and a half miles. For the rest of the hike, you get to enjoy ridgetop views of Giles County and West Virginia while hiking level ground or descending. Cascading Mill Creek is a lively traveling partner for the last mile.

The Lowdown

The climb to Angel's Rest above Pearisburg is notorious among southbound Appalachian Trail hikers for its punishing incline. Yes, you must endure a one-and-a-half-mile, 1,650-foot climb before you can sprawl over a boulder enjoying Giles County from a heavenly perspective. But the ascent has its own rewards. Noise and heat fall away as you zigzag up the slope, moving from thick poplar and oak to laurel and rhododendron. The spring you thought was finished revives in azaleas, fire pinks, and lady slippers at 3,770 feet. And fall starts creeping over the summit in mid-September with the first red woodbine and yellow nut trees.

Angel's Rest looms over Pearisburg. From almost anywhere in town, it's easy to determine whether a patch of clouds is resting on the tip of Pearis Mountain. When it is, natives say, "The angel is in."

To reach Angel's Rest and the Appalachian Trail, take Horsley Drive one block downhill from Linda Lorraine's to Wenonah Street and head right toward Angel's Rest. You'll pass the town pool, the pillared Senator Shumate house, a supermarket, and a block of shops before intersecting with Main Street at the courthouse. Turn right, go three blocks, and turn left on Johnson Avenue. Take the first left (Morris Avenue) and go about six-tenths of a mile until you see a tree bearing the white AT blaze and a path entering the forest on the left.

Key at-a-Glance Information

Length: 8.5 miles

Difficulty: Demanding; mountains bikers have named the section of this hike from the AT down to Mill Creek "the Wheezer"

Elevation gain and loss: 1,650-feet

Scenery: Stupendous views of Pearisburg, Narrows, the New River, Wilburn Valley, and Mill Creek's rapids

Exposure: Shady–85   Exposed–15

Solitude: Some weekend traffic on the AT; near perfect on the Wheezer

Surface: Dirt path and U.S. Forest Service road

Trail markings: Appalachian Trail is well marked; double-track path for Wheezer, single track for Catwalk

Author's hiking time: 5 hours

Season: All seasons, but avoid the November hunting season

Access: No permits or fees

Maps: U.S. Forest Service map of Jefferson National Forest, Blacksburg Ranger District

Other uses for trail: AT is for hiking only; mountain biking is gnarly but allowed on Wheezer and Catwalk.

Facilities: None on trail; food at Pearisburg and Narrows

Shuttle: Innkeepers will help you shuttle your car before your hike or take you back to your car the next morning, but you need to make your request with your reservation.

Lodging info:

Linda Lorraine's Bed and Breakfast, 1409 Cabot Drive, Pearisburg, VA; (540) 921-2069; www.lindalorraines.com; $$–$$$$

New River Inn, 307 Main Street, Narrows, VA; (540) 726-2770; www.abebooks.com/home/booknbed; $

Alternative lodging:

Rendezvous Motel (call (540) 921-2636), Plaza Motel (call (540) 921-2591), and Holiday Motor Lodge (call (540) 921-1551), all in Pearisburg within a half mile of the trail.

Angel's Rest offers a lofty perspective of Giles County.

The sense of escape is immediate. You enter into a tight, close bower of greenery and branches; the sky is not visible again until near the summit. The vegetation lining the trail is so uniform for the first two-tenths of a mile it seems landscaped. Don't examine that border too closely; the shiny, three-leafed vine is poison ivy. The herb with jagged leaves is stinging nettle—reputedly great in potions, but its prickers can give your legs a rash.

The well-worn trail leads into a spring-fed ravine and briefly along an old logging road before settling into a consistent, thrashing course of switchbacks. The path crosses over two ancient rock slides. Watch the feet; a spring seeps under one, making the rocks slippery, and the terrain snake-friendly.

In a dozen treks up this trail, I have yet to spot a snake. Millipedes are another story. I have never climbed Pearis Mountain without seeing one of these sightless little creatures tapping its way across the ground with its antennae. Like snakes, they coil up when they feel threatened. But instead of striking, millipedes form roly-poly balls to present their hard exoskeletons and protect their more vulnerable undersides. If you continue to mess with them, some will emit a noxious secretion. But don't harass them; they are some of nature's best composters and as harmless as the dead leaves and wood they feed upon.

Gradually, the thriving hardwood forest of the lowlands gives way to stunted oaks and shrubs. When you reach the boulders at the top, detour a few hundred feet to the right on a blue-blazed trail for a view of

Pearisburg and the twisting New River. The AT continues to the crest of Angel's Rest and follows along a rock ledge overhanging Wilburn Valley for more spectacular views.

Now you're coasting. The trail is flat, and only downhills lie ahead. After about one and a half miles through ferns and heath shrubs along the ridge, the landscape opens up under a power line with good views of Wilburn Valley. From here, the AT descends about 200 feet and turns left. At this juncture, turn right to follow an as-yet unblazed forest service road known as "the Wheezer" among mountain bikers. If you were coming from Narrows, you'd know why.

Wheezer is a grassy double-track, bordered by mountain laurel and flame azaleas at its higher elevations. As its downward slope increases, you'll see what local mountain bikers describe as "babyheads," treacherous loose stones along its eight-switchback descent. You plunge about 1,100 feet in the last half mile before Mill Creek.

Forty miles of unmarked trails fan out from the Mill Creek area. Several take off from Wheezer on the way down Pearis Mountain. Ignore these other trails unless you have ample time and energy to explore. Continue down the double-track Wheezer and veer right when another double track comes in from the left. At Mill Creek, you will reach the pond that was once the town reservoir for Narrows.

However, if you'd like an intimate half-mile alternative to the double track, look for a small path exiting on the left side of the sixth switchback. Follow this trail on an overgrown logging road to a cobbled path along Mill Creek's waterfalls and pocket pools of pink-fleshed native trout. This path, Catwalk, is a super technical, rocky, crazy descent for a biker, but only mildly pulse-quickening for a hiker.

Someone started a tradition of creating rock cairns along Catwalk, and now its course is marked with carefully balanced Buddhist shrines. Ralph Robertson, a local outdoorsman and guide, makes a habit of stacking a new rock on one of the towers each time he passes through. "A cairn represents life," he says. "It's real tippy, but every now and then someone comes along and adds a new piece to it."

Robertson offers New River Inn guests the opportunity to go on local expeditions with him, giving them grounding in the cultural history of Narrows. "This area used to be called Hungry Holler, but after awhile the town didn't think that sounded good, so they changed it to Monte Vista," Robertson says. "The whole place was logged out 60 years ago, and you know what happens to the soil after a clear cut. When a thunderstorm hit back here, folks couldn't sleep for the sound of rocks pinging around off the banks. Good thing those banks are covered now."

Hemlocks, beech, hickories, and oaks shelter the trail, and trilliums, jack-in-the pulpits, ferns, and ramps—the garlicky spring tonic of the southern Appalachians—grow in profusion from the dark earth.

Robertson has seen bears farther up the creek, and, when he has searched under rocks, rattlesnakes.

Catwalk and Wheezer converge at the pond that was once the reservoir. Town employees and visiting college students have been working to build a path along the left side of Mill Creek, but no bridge has been completed as of summer 2000, so it's best to take the forest road downhill a quarter mile to the completed bridge on the left. Cross there and make a quick right. In spring, you'll see at least a dozen species of wildflowers—from the first hepatica and coltsfoot blossoms in March to Bowman's root and mayapple in May.

The path leads to Poplar Street Bridge. Step right over the bridge and make an immediate left onto Northview Street, which goes about a mile to Main Street. Turn left on Main Street and you'll see the New River Inn on the right in a quarter mile. A good dinner spot is Anna's Restaurant, a block west at the end of Main Street. Get a seat near the window so you can see Wolf Creek and Pearis Mountains to the south and Peters Mountain standing guard in the north. "Paradise—I think we're in it," says Robertson.

Linda Lorraine's Bed and Breakfast
Pearisburg, Virginia

From Linda Lorraine's porch, her dining room, and most of the guest rooms in her 1908 Georgian-style house, you can eyeball Angel's Rest—that great heap of mountain you must climb on this hike. Linda Lorraine Jametsky can no longer visually make out Angel's Rest, but she knows her way around her kitchen well enough to cook up a breakfast that's a worthy send-off. Although she's an expert in concocting low-fat, sugar-free items, she has enough Southern blood to do justice to biscuits and gravy with eggs. Her husband, Ron, makes French toast angelica for the Angel's Rest bound. And if that's not enough, anything in the guest refrigerator is up for grabs. "This is your home away from home," Linda says.

The Jametskys start priming hikers for their big walk the evening before with low-fat brownies or blueberry cobbler. They can do a boxed lunch if you give them a day's notice.

Unlike most other bed-and-breakfasts, Linda Lorraine's welcomes children and outdoor dogs. Two of the spacious bedrooms have two queen beds to accommodate families.

The four upstairs bedrooms are served by large shared bathrooms, one for men and one for women. Rooms are supplied with robes, an amenity inspired by Linda's midnight encounter in the hall with a nude guest. "I'm not that blind," she says. "But I can pretend."

Furniture is an eclectic blend of semiformal sideboards, overstuffed chairs, and art deco dressers. Linda is likely to serve breakfast in a caftan; Ken in blue jeans. "We're not pretentious people," Linda says. "I think we get more done that way."

New River Inn and Bookstore
Narrows, Virginia

The New River Inn and Bookstore got its start two years ago when Narrows newcomer Diana Fields decided she wouldn't commute to work. Shortly after she made that decision, the house next door to her went up for sale during the same week when she had an opportunity to buy 5,000 books for $250. The bookstore and bed-and-breakfast were born. Fields and her partner, Mickey Branyon, provide a shuttle service for Appalachian Trail hikers coming off the trail for supplies. Occasionally lame or cashless hikers enthusiastically trade painting, cleaning, and other labor for lodging.

The New River Inn consists of three upstairs bedrooms and one downstairs—comfortable, unpretentious rooms with pretty bedspreads

and antique furniture. A clawfoot tub in the shared bathroom invites long soaks, perhaps accompanied by a cup of the inn's apricot ginger or Egyptian licorice tea. And guests have their choice of 10,000 books for night reading.

The couple loves catering to hikers and other ecotourists. Their latest move has been to acquire another downtown Narrows building, so that they can move the bookstore, expand the bed-and-breakfast, and open a canoe and tubing livery.

Virginia Beach

Beach to Bay

This hike leads from the beach at Ramada Plaza Resort Oceanfront to Virginia Beach Resort, through First Landing State Park's wildest wetland trails, along Broad Bay, past tea-colored swamps, and over sandy bayside beaches.

The Lowdown

You're always within Virginia Beach city limits on this hike, but once you slip into the moss-draped forest of First Landing State Park, it's easy to forget Virginia's most populous city. To get there from the Ramada, walk out to the sidewalk along Atlantic Avenue (US 60) and head right for seven blocks. At 64th Street, cross Atlantic and head left a block to the park entrance. As soon as you enter the paved road through the gate, the atmosphere cools and moistens. Sounds of distant traffic become muted in the pine needles and swamp bay.

Continue on the paved road almost a mile after entering the park. Long Creek Trail leaves the roadway to the right on an orange-blazed, sandy path. Go three-tenths of a mile on Long Creek before taking the green-blazed Osprey Trail, which shoots off to the left. This path is narrow and more aquatic, and you must time your hike to not coincide with high tide (call the park at (757) 481-2131). A sign at the trailhead warns, "May Flood in High Tide." (A message scratched under the official one advises, "So Go Nude." I don't think so—too much poison ivy along the trail.) If the Osprey Trail is flooded, return to the Long Creek Trail and continue on it, past where the Osprey Trail rejoins it at White Hall Lake.

Shortly after you turn onto the Osprey Trail, you start seeing water. Tea-colored ponds stand under the swamp bay thickets. Swamps with

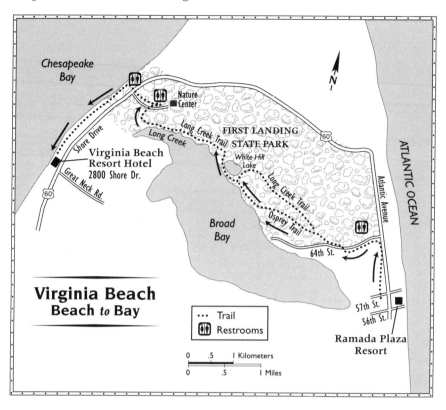

Getting there:

Exit Interstate 64 at US 13 and then take a right turn on US 60 (Shore Drive). Go about three and a half miles, cross Lynnhaven Inlet, and look for the Virginia Beach Resort Hotel on the left across from Great Neck Road.

To reach the Ramada Plaza Resort Oceanfront, continue around the point on US 60 (which becomes Atlantic Avenue) and look for the first tall hotel on the left.

Key at-a-Glance Information

Length: 8.4 miles

Difficulty: Easy, mostly flat

Elevation gain: Minimal rise and fall on forested dunes just above sea level

Scenery: Lush forest, marsh, bay, and ocean

Exposure: Shady–60   Moderate–10   Exposed–30

Solitude: Least used trails in park, but may see 5 to 25 other people on summer weekends

Surface: Hard-packed dirt through park, paved on bike route, open beach

Trail markings: Long Creek Trail is orange blazed; Osprey Trail green; and broad Cape Henry Trail requires no blazes

Author's hiking time: 4 hours

Season: Year-round

Access: No fees or permits unless you leave your car at First Landing State Park (parking fee is $1–3 per day; no overnight parking unless you are camping at the beach)

Maps: Virginia Beach map and First Landing State Park Trail System map, available at park visitors centers and at Virginia Beach Resort Hotel's fitness center

Other uses for trail: Cape Henry Trail through park is also a bike trail; other park trails are off-limits to bikes.

Facilities: Bathrooms at Bayside and Forest Visitors' Centers and at 64th Street entrance to the park

Shuttle: Virginia Beach Resort Hotel will shuttle guests back to their cars, but please make these arrangements a day or two in advance.

Lodging info:

Ramada Plaza Resort Oceanfront, Oceanfront at 57th Street, Virginia Beach, Virginia; (757) 428-7025; (800) 365-3032; www.ramada.com; $$–$$$$$

Virginia Beach Resort Hotel and Conference Center, 2800 Shore Drive, Virginia Beach, Virginia; (757) 481-9000; (800) 468-2722; www.virginia beachresort.com; $$–$$$$$

Alternative lodging:

For First Landing State Park's cabins (two-night minimum), call (800) 933-PARK. For other hotel options, call the Virginia Beach Visitors' Center at (757) 437-4888.

Osprey, egrets, and other fowl are often spotted along First Landing State Park's Long Creek Trail.

islands of delicate royal ferns appear as you approach the bay. You can smell salt in the air.

The closer you get to the bay, the more Spanish moss drapes from the trees. This is as far north as you'll find this semitropical epiphyte and as far south as you'll see some of the temperate zone plants. Many people mistake Spanish moss for a parasite such as mistletoe. But Spanish moss is no free-loader on the trees' nutrient systems. Like other epiphytes, it draws its sustenance from the air and from rainwater running down the tree bark.

The prickly pear cactus found along this trail just yards from the Spanish moss illustrates the diversity of flora found at First Landing. Both grow from a high, shrubby sand dune as the trail approaches Broad Bay.

The park is home to 23 species of mammals, 71 types of trees, 150 species of birds, and more than 48 varieties of amphibians and reptiles. If you are very lucky, you will see an endangered chicken turtle with its amazingly extendible neck.

Although two species of poisonous snakes live here—the cotton-mouth and the copperhead—they aren't likely to be slithering anywhere near the trail. Ticks, mosquitoes, and chiggers are much more likely to menace you, beginning in late May and continuing through summer. Park volunteer Byron Babcock advises protecting yourself by wearing long pants and light clothes (so the ticks can be easily spotted) and spraying yourself liberally with repellent.

Mosquitoes are a common pest in the park, but another denizen of the swamps, the dragonfly, keeps them in check. How many mosquitoes can a dragonfly put away? One University of Pennsylvania researcher observed that a dragonfly larva consumed 3,201 mosquito larvae over the course of its life—and that wasn't even counting the number of flying insects it ate as an adult.

As I rested on a rotting log along Osprey Trail, I watched two dragonflies strike and consume at least a dozen flying termites. The dragonflies gobbled their prey while wheeling around in midair to attack their next victims. Farther down the trail, I examined a dead green darner before ants finished dismantling it. Its legs were clustered right behind the mouthparts and they bowed out, forming a basket to catch prey and shoot the hapless critters into its mouth. Dragonflies' legs are so adapted for feeding that they are no longer able to use the crooked appendages for walking.

As you follow the trail, Broad Bay, that wide body of water on your left, will segue into wide Long Creek without obvious punctuation. During low tide, the muddy marshes are littered with barnacles and mussels. True to its name, the trail leads you past several osprey nests perched atop dead trees. These fish hawks return in pairs to the same nests each year.

Long Creek Trail rejoins Osprey Trail on a dune near White Hill Lake, another good spot for wildlife watching. Besides the two permanent osprey nests, the lake is home to an American bittern and a couple of kingfishers. Gray foxes have been spotted robbing the nests here.

A viewing platform near the intersection with Kingfisher Trail produced a wildlife bonanza for me one April morning. Not only did I see three osprey having territory issues over a nest, but I spied a bittern, an egret, and a raccoon. Even the moments between sightings seemed full. Rustling marsh grass has a presence; it sounds like a whisper and an expectation.

The streams that enter the bay are as black as used motor oil due to tannic acid from decaying pine needles and cypress bark. As the trail continues north, Long Creek narrows so much that homes on the other side are within pinecone lobbing distance. Wild yuccas, willow oaks, and wild pinks, whose lazy stems leave the blossoms lying face up, grow in the sandy soil beside the creek.

After curving away from the creek over forested dunes, the trail soon hits the park driveway. Turn left and cross Shore Drive to First Landing's Chesapeake Bay Center museum and aquariums. The center features an extensive display interpreting the lives of the 144 men who landed their three small ships at Cape Henry in 1607 and became the first European colonists in this country. You also can learn about how their arrival ultimately changed tidewater forests and the Chesapeake Bay.

After touring the center, take the boardwalk behind the building out to the ocean. You can reach the Virginia Beach Resort Hotel and Conference Center, the first multistoried building on the left, by walking a mile down the beach.

Ramada Plaza Resort Oceanfront
Virginia Beach, Virginia

The Ramada Plaza Oceanfront's claim to distinction is its distance—about a half mile—from the pack of other hotels that vie for space along Virginia Beach's Boardwalk. This beach doesn't have the crowds, the noise, or the bustling retail district at its back. It's billed as a place to relax.

Like other chain hotels, the Ramada offers rooms that are predictably clean, comfortable, and well supplied. Most of the 245 rooms and suites offer a view of the ocean, and all are equipped with refrigerators, microwaves, coffee pots, hair driers, and data ports.

If the beach isn't enough to entertain you, there's an indoor-outdoor pool, a hot tub, a fitness center, volleyball nets, and a restaurant named as one of the country's 50 best for seafood. A pub offers lighter fare.

Rates vary drastically with the season; room prices in November through March, often great hiking weather, are almost one-third those of the summer season.

Virginia Beach Resort Hotel and Conference Center
Virginia Beach, Virginia

On the bay side of Virginia Beach, waves are gentle, bars are scarce, and a lightly developed expanse of beach extends all the way to First Landing State Park. The city's sole bayside hotel, Virginia Beach Resort capitalizes on these characteristics with the family and conference crowd.

Although shops and eateries operate year-round in the neighborhood, the resort provides options for guests who want to dine and play without leaving the premises. Three restaurants provide casual and fine dining, and a deli will pack box lunches for hikers.

Guests have free access to a health club, an indoor/outdoor swimming pool, a whirlpool, volleyballs, bicycles, outdoor tennis courts, and a children's activity camp. The adventuresome can cloister themselves in a darkened cubicle to try out the HydroSonic Ultrasound Relaxation System. A vibrating waterbed combines with a surround sound system to give a massage from the inside out.

The hotel is designed so that each of the 295 suites has a balcony view of the bay. Guests can watch the sun rise over the distant ocean and set behind the Chesapeake Bay Bridge.

The hotel's ownership is unique in that private individuals own 40 percent of the suites. Owners' tastes are not reflected in the rooms' decor, but some staff members feel that guests treat the facilities with a little more care knowing that the owner could be someone like themselves. These owners are allowed to use the suites two weeks each year and receive rental checks annually.

A paved bike path, only half a block away, runs parallel with Shore Drive from First Landing State Park. Maps are available from the fitness center.

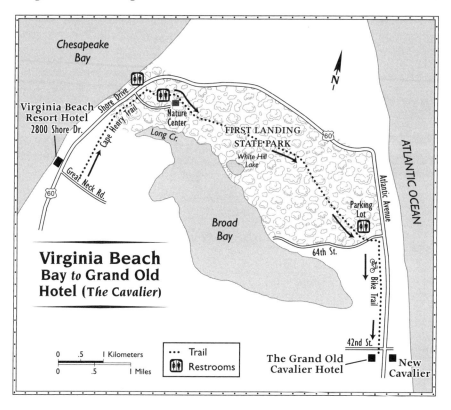

Getting there:

Exit Interstate 64 at US 13 and then take a right turn on US 60 (Shore Drive). Go about 3.5 miles, cross Lynnhaven Inlet, and look for the hotel on the left across from Great Neck Road.

To reach the Cavalier, continue around the point on US 60 (which becomes Atlantic Avenue) several miles to 42nd Street.

Virginia Beach

Bay to Grand Old Hotel

This walk travels along a residential bike path and through First Landing State Park's lush forest and swamps to a grand old hotel, The Cavalier.

The Lowdown

Virginia Beach is supposed to have the jump on spring weather and the hold on balmy autumns. And yet there I was in April (while friends 2 hours west enjoyed 70° barbecue weather) being lashed by 35-mph winds, horizontal rain, and hand-numbing 50° temperatures—bad weather for beach walking, but very invigorating for a hike through First Landing State Park's forest. The spring green was ratcheted up to lime neon, and the frogs, raccoons, and egrets were reconnoitering a habitat newly rearranged by the northeaster. Above the squish, squish, squish of my own feet, I heard a kingfisher's wild laughter. The park was mine for the day.

This hike starts out like a typical city walk; you cross busy Shore Drive in front of the Virginia Beach Resort Hotel and stroll past a small shopping center on the left side of Great Neck Road to an asphalt path (an extension of the park's Cape Henry Trail, known simply as the bike route). Turn left and pass through flowering backyards (one resident has even set out small statues for your admiration), a neighborhood park, and over several neighborhood streets. You will reach the gates of First Landing State Park in about a mile.

Then things start getting wild. Ferns—chain fern, Goldie's fern, cinnamon fern—crowd next to the paved trail. Unseen amphibians and rep-

Key at-a-Glance Information

Length: 8.2 miles

Difficulty: Flat and easy

Elevation gain: Negligible

Scenery: Cypress swamp, hardwood forest, and city street with some views of the ocean

Exposure: Shady–70   Exposed–30

Solitude: Busy on weekends, except in winter

Surface: Paved into park and on bike route; hard-packed dirt through park

Trail markings: Dark green blazes on the Cape Henry Trail; bike routes are asphalt paths with line marking.

Author's hiking time: 4 hours

Season: Year-round

Access: No permits or fees unless you park your car at First Landing State Park (parking fee is $1–3; no overnight parking)

Maps: Virginia Beach map and *First Landing State Park Trail System Guide* available at park visitors centers and at Virginia Beach Resort Hotel fitness center

Other uses for trail: Bikes are allowed on Cape Henry Trail.

Facilities: Park bathrooms at 64th Street entrance and forest visitors' center

Shuttle: Virginia Beach Resort Hotel will shuttle guests back to their cars, but please make these arrangements a day or two in advance.

Lodging info:

Virginia Beach Resort Hotel and Conference Center, 2800 Shore Drive, Virginia Beach, Virginia; (757) 481-9000; (800) 468-2722; www.virginia beachresort.com; $$–$$$$$

The Cavalier, 42nd Street & Atlantic Avenue, Virginia Beach, Virginia; (757) 425-8555; (800) 446-8199; www.cavalier.hotel.com; $$$–$$$$$$

Alternative lodging:

For First Landing State Park's cabins (two-night minimum), call (800) 933-PARK. For other hotel options, call the Virginia Beach Visitors Center at (757) 437-4888.

tiles splash in the murky water of seeps and sloughs as you walk past. Four dozen species of amphibians and reptiles live here, including the poisonous cottonmouth and copperhead. You aren't likely to see these snakes if you stay on the trail, nor are the chances good you'll see the endangered chicken turtle with its amazingly extendible neck. But if you visit between Memorial Day and Labor Day, you are likely to encounter the park's major menaces—mosquitoes and ticks. Wear long pants and bring a good supply of strong bug repellent.

Soon after you enter First Landing you'll see a picnic area on the left. Follow Cape Henry Trail, still paved, across the paved vehicle road and through another seven-tenths of a mile of forest to the visitors' center. There you can use the restrooms, fill your water bottle, get a map, and learn more about the species of plants and animals found in this 2,770-acre park.

As you approach the visitors' center clearing, look toward the left for a circular mound with rocks and plantings facing in four directions. This is a burial pit for 64 Chesapeake Indians whose remains were found during local excavations. On the 390th anniversary of the settlers' 1607 arrival, the Indians' bones were returned to Mother Earth in a Native American ceremony.

The Chesapeakes were exterminated by the Powhatans, Pocahontas's tribe, as a proactive move after the Powhatan chief dreamed of being dominated by men from the east. Wrong men; fatal mistake. The dominating men, of course, were the descendants of John Smith, Christopher Newport, and other founders of Jamestown, the first permanent English-speaking settlement in the New World. These colonists first touched land just east of the park at Cape Henry. In commemoration, the park changed its name from Seashore to First Landing State Park in 1999.

To help visitors identify local plants, park volunteer Byron Babcock has transplanted many native plants into a garden in front of the visitors center. He can tell you which one was used as a hallucinogen and purgative by adolescent Indian boys during their vision quest and which has more caffeine than coffee. First Landing is an unusual blend of semitropical species (such as Spanish moss) in their northern-most habitat and some temperate-zone plants at the tip of their southern range.

The Cape Henry Trail strikes into the dune forest at the end of the visitors' center parking lot. Continue on this trail, or take the half-mile detour on the red-blazed Bald Cypress Trail to explore the swamp. It is well worth your time. The trail loops back to intersect again with the Cape Henry Trail less than a quarter mile from the visitors' center.

The Bald Cypress Trail sets out on boardwalks, and soon you're surrounded by cola-colored water and cypress trees hung in Spanish moss. Like tea brewed from leaves, the tannins in pine needles and cypress bark

*First Landing State Park trails lead through
cypress swamps.*

have leached out, giving the water its dark color. Because of the acidity, this water contains fewer bacteria and other microscopic life forms than most other water sources. In colonial times, water from these swamps was taken aboard ships because it stayed potable on long voyages.

The bald cypresses growing in the water get their name from the fact that, unlike true cypress trees, they lose their leaves every fall. The knobby knees poking through the water near the cypress trunks either help support the tree or aid it in taking in oxygen, depending upon which scientist you ask.

The oldest cypresses are more than 500 years old, but the land they stand on is very young—3,000 to 5,000 years old, as compared with the 200 million years the Blue Ridge Mountains have been around. Before the Cape Henry area was formed, the East Coast was a big valley made by the Susquehanna River. Ice melted; the sea rose higher; and the former valley was filled with water. A large sand spit was deposited in the Virginia Beach/Hampton Roads area where the river met the ocean.

As you rejoin the Cape Henry Trail and head left, you start to leave behind the shallow swamp and its cypress, black gum, and osmanthus (wild olive) trees and begin seeing more holly, loblolly pines, and grasses. The area looks much as it did almost 300 years ago, when Captain John Smith said, "Heaven and Earth never agreed better to frame a place for man's habitat."

Despite Smith's praise, Cape Henry remained uninhabited because its swamps and sand ridges were unsuitable for farming. Although the Chesapeake Indians used it for hunting and even established a hunting camp on Broad Bay, they referred to the area as "The Great Desert" because no one lived here permanently. The tradition continued with the colonists. In the early 1770s, fishermen from Princess Anne petitioned to keep the land in common ownership to preserve their rights to camp and haul nets there. In 1869, it became state property, and in 1936, it opened as a state park.

Tales of pirate treachery on this land have been partially corroborated by journals and courthouse records. As the story goes, Blackbeard's lookout crew would hide in the top branches of a tall tree near the shore. When they spied a merchant ship, they rushed down and sent smoke signals to their mates aboard a ship hidden in the cove. After robbing the hapless merchant, the pirates would come ashore in the semitropical forest. According to legend, they buried fortunes in gold coins and jewels in the dunes. No evidence of the booty remains, and digging in the park is prohibited.

The trail becomes more sylvan the further west you go. Oak, hickory, beech, and loblolly pines tower above bamboo, sweet bay, and a rare scrub species of live oak. Flowers include dogwood, yellow jessamine, and partridgeberry in spring and, in the summer, yellow orchids, butterfly peas, sourwood, trumpet creeper, and false foxglove.

Along the way, Cape Henry Trail moves past intersections with Kingfisher Trail and White Hill Lake Trail before it crosses over 64th Street, where you will turn left and go two blocks to Atlantic Avenue. From here, you can continue on a bike route to your lodging on 42nd Street. Or you can turn left on Atlantic Avenue to visit the Association for Research and Enlightenment (ARE), which offers spa services on 66th Street for post-hike pampering. I'd pass on the colonic hydrotherapy that psychic Edgar Cayce occasionally recommended and order a therapeutic touch massage instead.

The ARE houses information on ESP, dreams, holistic health, meditation, and life after death. Although Edgar Cayce, its founder and the country's best-known psychic, died over 50 years ago, visitors still seek out his predictions and prescriptions in the ARE library.

The ARE Visitor Center also offers an ESP tester for judging one's telepathy, a bookstore designed according to feng shui principles, and a meditation room overlooking the ocean. Guided tours are available seven days a week; free meditation classes and an ESP demonstration are offered on weekends.

But the main draw for hikers is the half-day spa package offered by the ARE Health Services Center. Massages seem to simultaneously stimulate and relax the recipient, and you may emerge from the session with the sensation you are running without friction. Massage therapists say the bodywork strengthens the immune system and improves lymph circulation. Some of us simply feel more relaxed. For appointments, call (757) 437-7202.

The Cavalier is located near the Beach's Boardwalk district. When you are rested, you might want to stroll south along the beach, stopping off at the city's smaller museums. Just off the Boardwalk on 24th Street, you can step back in time at the Old Coast Guard Station. Learn about wrecks that occurred off the Virginia Beach coast and zoom in on passing ships via a roof-mounted video camera. A short walk down the Boardwalk is the Atlantic Wildfowl Heritage Museum. Entering this turn-of-the-century cottage on the oceanfront at 12th Street is like being transported to one of the old hunt clubs that previously dotted Virginia Beach waterways. Inside is a collection of prized decoys dating from ancient times up to the present. Or you might just want to stroll up and down the three-mile Boardwalk, enjoying the ocean.

Virginia Beach Resort Hotel and Conference Center
Virginia Beach, Virginia

On the bay side of Virginia Beach, waves are gentle, bars are scarce, and the beach is uncrowded all the way to First Landing State Park. The city's sole bayside hotel, Virginia Beach Resort capitalizes on these characteristics to serve families and the conference crowd.

Although shops and eateries operate year-round in the neighborhood, the resort provides options for guests who want to dine and play without leaving the premises. Three restaurants provide casual and fine dining and a deli will pack box lunches for hikers.

Guests have free access to a health club, an indoor/outdoor swimming pool, a whirlpool, volleyballs, bicycles, outdoor tennis courts, and a free children's activity camp. Theme parties are occasionally held for guests in the beachside cabana. If you're daring, you can cloister yourself in a darkened cubicle to try out the HydroSonic Ultrasound Relaxation System, a vibrating waterbed with a surround sound system that seems to massage you from the inside out.

The hotel is designed so that each of the 295 suites has a balcony view of the bay. Guests can watch the sun rise over the distant ocean and set behind the Chesapeake Bay Bridge.

A paved bike path, only half a block away, runs parallel with Shore Drive from First Landing State Park. Maps are available from the fitness center.

The Cavalier
Virginia Beach, Virginia

"The Cavalier" slips off the tongues of longtime Virginia Beach visitors, but the Cavalier is actually two hotels: the older Cavalier on the Hill and the newer Cavalier Oceanfront.

While the luxurious new Cavalier has all the modern conveniences, including computer modems in the lamps, the old Cavalier oozes genteel

charm from its floral carpet to its custom molding. It harks back to the 1920s when waiters wore white gloves, frequenters of the basement Hunt Club actually brought in game for the chefs to cook, and every bathtub had a fourth handle for salt water. The Cavalier was then the largest employer of big bands in the world. Over the years,

six U.S. presidents have laid their heads on the old Cavalier's pillows. Movies have been filmed here, stars have vacationed here, and, in a dark moment during Prohibition, brewery founder Adolph Coors plunged to his death here from a sixth floor window.

The hotel property now spans 18 well-groomed acres, which contain a health club, basketball courts, an outdoor aerobic fitness course, a putting green, tennis courts, shuffleboard courts, swimming pools, and a private beach. The hotel runs its own summer day camp, free to guests' children. Combined, the hotels offer 400 guest rooms, five restaurants, and a gift shop. The Cavalier could be a village.

While the weather forecaster won't guarantee sunshine from June 1 through August 31 at Virginia Beach, the Cavalier does. If a rainy day occurs on your visit, the hotel will issue a certificate for a complimentary night on a future stay within the year. The older Cavalier on the Hill is only open May through October, but the Cavalier Oceanfront carries on year-round.

As you might expect, the Cavalier is pricey in the summer, although some of its packages for couples reduce the sting considerably. Room rates in the November through March off-season are less than half the rates you'll pay in summer, and the old Cavalier is more economical than the oceanfront hotel.

The Virginia Creeper Trail

Green Cove to Abingdon

This two-day trek is mostly downhill from Green Cove, high on the knee of Whitetop Mountain, to Damascus, known as "Trail Town USA," and on to Abingdon. The 31-mile stretch traverses some of the prettiest gorges and pastoral scenery of the Southern Appalachians.

The Lowdown

The Virginia Creeper Trail follows the pathway of the old Virginia-Carolina Railroad, west 34.5 miles from Whitetop Station to Abingdon through some of the highest terrain of any Eastern rail-trail. For many years after it was constructed in 1900, the Virginia-Carolina was the only commercial means of getting iron ore and timber out of these high mountains.

Passengers affectionately dubbed the line the "Virginia Creeper" because of its slow crawl up the almost four-percent grade in the mountainous eastern half. After operating in the red since the Great Depression, the Creeper ran its last train in March 1977. The U.S. Forest Service and the towns of Abingdon and Damascus purchased the right-of-way to open the public trail in 1987. With about 26,000 users a year, the rail-trail sees more human traffic now than it did during its railroad years.

The trail leads over more than 60 bridges and trestles, two-thirds of them in the rugged eastern section. Around every bend, the Virginia Creeper gives your eyes beauty enough to revive your soul.

Mile for mile, the eastern section is an easy hike, but long. You go steadily downhill almost the entire 15 miles, on a curvy course that plays tag with the White Top Laurel Creek. The downhill plunge begins soon after you leave Buchanan Inn and head along a field, past a hillside where crows seem waiting to heckle the next owl or raptor.

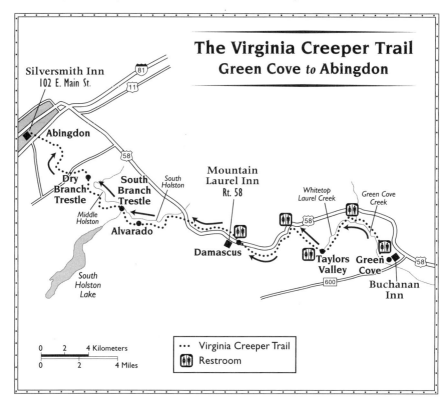

Getting there:

To reach Damascus, take US 58 eastward 10 miles from Exit 19 off Interstate 81. The Mountain Laurel Inn is on the right as you approach town. For Green Cove, follow the directions to Damascus and stay on US 58E though town into a sharp right turn and over the mountain to Green Cove. At the Christian Church, turn right onto Green Cove Road and go a quarter of a mile. Buchanan Inn is on the right. To reach Abingdon, take US 58 westward from Exit 17 off Interstate 81 to Main Street and turn right, passing Barter Theatre. The Silversmith is almost directly across from the theater. To find the trailhead, turn left off Main Street onto Pecan Street at traffic signal number three. The trail is on the left in about a quarter of a mile.

Key at-a-Glance Information

Length: Green Cove to Damascus: 15 miles; Damascus to Abingdon: 16 miles

Difficulty: Easy

Elevation loss: 1,300 feet

Scenery: Beautiful; crosses over gorges, follows a tumbling stream, and passes though rolling pastures and forest

Exposure: Shady–55   Moderate–25   Exposed–20

Solitude: Fair number of cyclists on weekends

Surface: Packed-dirt or gravel double-track

Trail markings: Signs at intersections

Author's hiking time: Green Cove to Damascus: 6 hours; Damascus to Abingdon: 7 hours

Season: All seasons

Access: No permits or fees

Maps: USGS quadrangles, Damascus, Konnarock, and Abingdon; *Guide to the Virginia Creeper Trail* available at Abingdon, Damascus, and Green Cove visitors' centers

Other Uses for Trail: Mountain biking, horseback riding, and cross-country skiing

Facilities: Bathrooms and drinks at Green Cove, Taylors Valley, Damascus, Alvarado (seasonal), and Abingdon

Shuttles: Blue Blaze (800) 475-5095, blueblaze@naxs.com; Virginia Creeper Trail (877) 475-5416, mro@naxs.com

Lodging Info:

Buchanan Inn at Green Cove Station, 41261 Green Cove Road, Damascus, Virginia; (540) 388-3367; (877) 300-9328; $$

Mountain Laurel Inn, 22750 Jeb Stuart Highway (Highway 58), Damascus, Virginia; (540) 465-596; (888) 684-6698; www.mountainlaurelinn.com; $$–$$$$

Silversmith Inn, 102 East Main Street, Abingdon, Virginia (540) 676-3924; (800) 533-0195; www.bbhost.com/silversmithinn; $$$$

Alternative lodging:

In Green Cove, Buchanan Inn is the only place that serves dinner, but the Green Cove Inn (call (540) 388-3479) does have a kitchen. In Damascus, there's the Lazy Fox Inn (call (540) 475-5838), Apple Tree Bed and Breakfast (call (800) 231-7626), and Maples (call (540) 475-3943). Contact the Abingdon Convention and Visitors Bureau (call (800) 435-3440) for information about the town's 20 bed-and-breakfasts, hotels, and motels.

*The Virginia Creeper Trail leads over 60
bridges and trestles.*

Before you leave Green Cove though, you should visit Green Cove station. Inside, time seems to stand still; in front of a potbellied stove, hikers and bikers pass the time as rail travelers did a century ago. The only original depot left on the Creeper Trail, the Green Cove station has been reincarnated as a visitors' center/museum/snack bar. When photographer O. Winston Link traveled the country in the 1950s, capturing images of the last steam trains, he kept returning to the Virginia Creeper. Link's most popular photograph, "Maude Bows to the Virginia Creeper," shows a cart horse that seems to be paying homage to the mechanical behemoth. "Maude" and several other of Link's images hang on the walls of the depot.

From May through October, forest-service volunteers sell snacks and answer your questions at the depot. Public restrooms are located behind the station, and you can fill your water bottle at the water fountain next door at the Green Cove Senior Center.

If you feel challenged to go to the trail's eastern terminus, you can make the seven-mile out-and-back trip to Whitetop, but be aware that it will add almost four hours to your hike.

As you ramble down the hill beyond Green Cove station (at about mile 30.5), you pass apple, sassafras, and oak. Green Cove Creek, which babbles through Buchanan Inn's yard, splashes below you for the next three miles. Near milepost 28.5, a pre-Cambrian fossil, one of the world's oldest, was found along a dirt road.

As you pass though stands of hemlocks and wildflowers, look for the rare painted trilliums found here in the spring. Green-white water cascades through Green Cove Gorge. You'll find very good viewing spots from boulders along the way.

The Appalachian Trail (AT) joins the Creeper to cross the 540-foot Luther Hassinger Memorial Trestle over the confluence of Green Cove and Whitetop Laurel Creeks. At milepost 26.6, the AT veers off into the forest again, but the Creeper stays on the double track for a view of a waterfall in a quarter mile. In the next three and a third miles, you cross six bridges over waterfalls and rocky cascades, through a section with 1,000-foot rock walls.

Whitetop Laurel is a free-stone stream—it is slightly acidic and doesn't produce the heavy mayfly hatches you see on limestone creeks like the Jackson. That doesn't prevent the Whitetop Laurel from being arguably the best wild trout stream in Virginia. The scenery is outstanding and the competition limited. Although much of the native brook-trout population was destroyed by careless logging practices in the 1920s, the rainbow trout that were once stocked here are now reproducing on their own. There is good fishing between mileposts 27 and 18.

The trail crosses a trestle over the creek near milepost 23 to enter the time-warp community of Taylors Valley. You cut across private front yards and back pastures, past Black Angus that won't give up their turf in the middle of the path. Go around them; they're bigger than you are and seem to have a surly recognition that you're a rung up on the food chain.

A railroad caboose serves as the Taylors Valley community center and picnic area. Bathrooms and a soda machine are located there.

Follow the stream as it meanders through a mostly evergreen forest. The trail parallels US 58 for more than four miles, although hikers are shielded by forest and the sound of water rippling over boulders. Near milepost 21 you reach the Straight Branch parking lot, picnic tables, fireplaces, and another juncture with the AT.

You'll cross four bridges on the next two-mile stretch of trail; the fourth is Iron Bridge, where you leave National Forest land for the last time. Soon, while the AT stays with US 58, the Creeper Trail forks left into Damascus to cross Laurel and Beaverdam Creeks.

Despite its rather scrubby appearance on the eastern end, Damascus is a gem of a town, the friendliest on the Appalachian Trail, according to the American Hiking Society. The Methodist Church provides a free hostel for AT hikers ($3 donation requested), and Callie's Restaurant and town hall have computers set up so you can keep friends and relatives apprised of your hiking progress. Damascus also has several bike shops, shuttle services, an outfitter, restaurants, and a variety of lodging.

You can reach the Mountain Laurel Inn by following the trail along US 58 west past the red caboose (an information center in season). At the statue garden, the trail ducks into a wooded area. You should cross US 58 and walk a quarter mile west to the Mountain Laurel's driveway.

Day Two

If you want to hike the more rolling riverside pastures and forest of the western half of the trail to Abingdon, you can start a second day of walking from Damascus. The trail leaves town along US 58 and Laurel Creek, which it parallels for the next three and a half miles. You pass through front yards, the back lot of a warehouse, and beside Iron Mountain Campground's cabins before crossing Routes 718, 715, and 1230. The trail goes under US 58 and hugs the banks of the slow-flowing South Fork of the Holston River through gated pastures. Much of the land is private; remember to close those gates so livestock doesn't escape and landowners don't decide to pasture their meanest bulls along the trail.

A bridge over Rockhouse Run takes you to the Alvarado (milepost 9), where a seasonal store operates out of the old post office. A railroad siding here once served a small sawmill. The railroad was proposed on the theory that Damascus was rich in iron ore (not rich enough, it turned out), but the line was actually completed when entrepreneurs realized they could make their fortune cutting the mountains' rich timber reserves.

African-American convicts from a state prison dug the railroad bed by hand, moving huge amounts of earth and stone. Some of the men died on the job and were buried in the right-of-way in unmarked graves, according to Norfolk and Western sources.

The highlight of this section's 15 bridges and trestles is the long span over the confluence of the South and Middle Forks of the Holston (milepost 8). The Middle Fork runs muddy from the rich limestone farmland to the northwest. The South Fork comes out of the Blue Ridge forests so clear that you can watch the progress of the two streams flowing together. They merge below the trestle to become the head of South Holston Lake.

Following the Middle Fork up a gorge, you'll see bloodroot, bellwort, Solomon's seal, mayapple, and other wildflowers making the most of the early spring light. Out in the fields at the top of the incline, fall flowers

The Virginia Creeper Trail is one of the highest rail-trails in the East.

such as purple ironweed, joe-pye weed, and black-eyed Susans make their stand.

The trail passes a sinkhole, old telegraph poles, and, near milepost 5, the trail's longest trestle. The Dry Branch Trestle curves 645 feet across a pasture. This area is called the River Knobs. These and the Great Knobs ahead are eroded remnants of siltstone and shale synclines that thrust up 250 feet above the valley. Between the two sets of knobs, you cross over Route 677 near the Watauga community.

Three trestles lift you over the Great Knobs, through more pasture, and you start seeing houses regularly. The trail crosses over the Glenrochie Country Club golf-course causeway and under Interstate 81. The large white brick house on the left was the home of former Virginia governor Wyndham Roberts, whose son and son-in-law served in the Civil War under Jeb Stuart.

Historic markers indicate the site of an old sawmill and a Y turn-around for the Virginia Creeper trains. The final trestle is at Green Springs Road. Across the street is a parking lot and the site of Black's Fort, which predated the Revolutionary War. You see no relics of the fort here; instead, Virginia Creeper Locomotive 433 sits in the parking lot, looking ready for another run.

Buchanan Inn at Green Cove Station
Green Cove, Virginia

The Buchanan Inn has been serving the public almost since it was built in 1915 for William and Mary Hart Buchanan. Mary put up 25 to 50 boxed lunches every day from 1920 until the 1960s for Norfolk and Western passengers and crew members on their way to West Jefferson, North Carolina. A typical lunch included ham biscuits, fried chicken, fresh tarts, and coffee in a Coke bottle. It was not uncommon for the Virginia Creeper train to be snowed in, and travelers would fill up all available floor space in the Buchanan home.

Guests no longer sleep on the floors and the fresh-brewed coffee isn't dispensed in Coke bottles, but the Buchanan Inn is again serving travelers on the Virginia Creeper. In 1999, the Buchanan's granddaughter, Annette, and her husband, Jim Goode, reopened the Buchanan Inn as a bed-and-breakfast, offering three renovated guest rooms with private baths. Neighbor and innkeeper Barbara Clark serves breakfast, afternoon tea, and occasional dinners to guests, using some of Mary Buchanan's recipes. Dinner is served by reservation only, so make your request with your room reservation.

Now that the train no longer clanks to a stop by the station in front of Buchanan Inn, the complete stillness of this remote community is something few modern people experience. Even cars are scarce, especially at night.

The rooms are named for the three Buchanan daughters, Adele, LaVaun, and Eleanor, and keep the character of an earlier time with period furniture. But concessions have been made to modern times—there are phone jacks in each room for computer access and a surround-sound television in the common area.

"Our goal is to continue the tradition of hospitality here," says Jim Goode, a retired chaplain. "We offer a warm place of charm, friendship, and good food."

Children are accommodated for an additional fee, and credit cards are accepted.

Mountain Laurel Inn
Damascus, Virginia

The Mountain Laurel Inn was built by one of Damascus' founding families, the Rambos; it took two years to complete, between 1901 and 1903. Most of this time was spent carving chestnut panels. All the rooms, even the bathrooms in this Queen Anne Victorian home, are paneled in fine, handcrafted chestnut cut from Washington County forests before the chestnut blight. When you lie in the Rambo suite, you look up at squares of the dark paneling over your head. The Rambos had lumber-business connections, it seems.

Damascus was a logging-boom town, but once the huge chestnuts, oak, and poplar had been logged out, the industry moved on and the town began to get pretty again. Now Damascus has a new identity as a trail town, and the Mountain Laurel Inn caters mainly to people who like their timber standing.

Jim and Nathalie Graham fell in love with the Mountain Laurel without knowing anything about its past or present. A retired military couple with experience running a London pub featuring Southern cooking, all the Grahams knew in 1999 was that they wanted this house. So they moved in their Estonian barber chair, their German merry-go-round horse, their painting once owned by Princess Di's dad, and set up innkeeping in the four upstairs bedrooms.

Nathalie soon found a benevolent ghost (though Jim remains skeptical), whose clattering footsteps are occasionally heard on the stairs. Jim and Nathalie have more than enough presence to fill up the house on their own. Nathalie is planning to move a mountain church to the garden for weddings. Jim, who once sang the national anthem for Atlanta Braves games and appeared regularly on the Don Ho Show, is likely to break into song while serving breakfast. Among his favorites are "Climb Every Mountain," "Unchained Melody," and "Moon River."

The singing is perfect accompaniment to a breakfast of French toast with Nathalie's special orange sauce, sausage, cereal, and wonderful coffee, all served under a crystal chandelier in the elegant dining room. Guests also have the run of a downstairs sitting room, first and second story porches, and three acres of lawn.

Silversmith Inn
Abingdon, Virginia

A silversmith once did live on the site of the Silversmith Inn, and host Rick Stevens has the spoon to prove it. The actual 1800 silver shop is long gone, but the charm of an earlier day lingers in this 1871 brick structure built over the foundation of Michael Shaver's shop.

The silver shop was destroyed by fire in 1856, and 14 years later, John Barr built the present three-story house on the foundation. He

eventually sold it to Stephen Jackson, founder of the Kappa Sigma fraternity. After Jackson's death in 1892, the building reincarnated as a rooming house for at least a decade.

The airy Barr Room, with its poplar plank floors and floor-to-ceiling shutters, is dedicated to the home's first owner, and the two-bedroom Shaver Suite pays homage to the silversmith. The poster beds and cherry furnishings would probably have pleased the skilled craftsman. In addition, the inn features a stately Judges Room, with bishop-style bed and fireplace, and a Chesapeake Suite with its own living room.

The inn is located adjacent to Barter Stage II, across the street from the main Barter Theater, and a block from the historic Martha Washington Hotel. More importantly, it's only a block and a half from the Virginia Creeper Trail.

With trail users in mind, the Stevens installed an outdoor hot tub on a shady side porch. There is also a secure bike storage area, in-house gym facilities, afternoon tea, and a piano and guitar ready to provide impromptu entertainment. The hot breakfasts are the best of Rick's years of experimentation with recipes for fruit muffins, quiches, egg casseroles, and other dishes.

The Washington & Old Dominion Rail-Trail

Leesburg to Hamilton

Pass through Leesburg's historical district, some pretty countryside, and good bird-watching territory on the way to Hamilton's old depot.

The Lowdown

The Washington and Old Dominion Railroad Regional Park is a 45-mile rail-trail extending from Alexandria northwest to Purcellville. For the last 30.5 miles, 2 trails run side by side—an asphalt passage that extends the whole 45 miles, and a shorter, dirt horsepath running in a parallel shaded area. Hikers are welcome on either. The trail slopes perceptibly uphill west of Leesburg. Because of the incline, early rail passengers nicknamed it the Virginia Creeper line—the same name as a truly mountainous rail-trail in southwest Virginia.

Norris House Inn, which got its start 90 years before the Washington & Old Dominion Railroad, sits in the heart of Leesburg's National Register Historic District. If you have any time before you start the day's hike, you should visit Loudoun Museum, a block east, and take the town walking tour. Leesburg is one of the best-preserved historic towns in the Virginias, with a recorded history dating from 1757. Exhibits include the journal of an Englishman visiting during the American Revolution, letters of newly emancipated slaves to their former masters, and examples of families split by the Civil War.

To reach the trail from Norris House Inn, go east on Londoun Street until you reach King Street, then turn right. The trail is two blocks south on King. Turn right to head toward Hamilton. If you're awake with the birds, you may want to do some serious bird-watching along the trail.

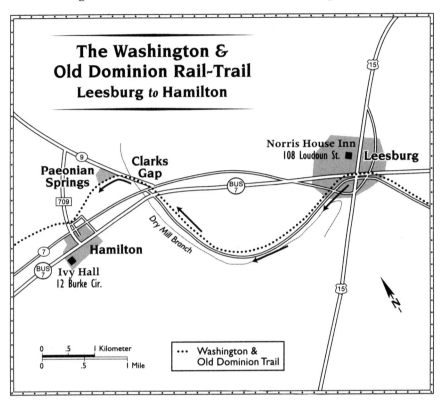

The Washington &
Old Dominion Rail-Trail
Leesburg *to* Hamilton

Norris House Inn
108 Loudoun St. ■ Leesburg

Clarks
Gap

Paeonian
Springs

Dry Mill Branch

Hamilton
Ivy Hall
12 Burke Cir.

| 0 | .5 | 1 Kilometer |
| 0 | .5 | 1 Mile |

··· Washington &
Old Dominion Trail

Getting there:

The Leesburg access to the trail can be reached by taking Route 7 into Leesburg, turning left onto Sycolin Road, and turning immediately right into the parking lot for the Douglass Community Center, where you can park at the rear of the building. The trail is behind the picnic area. Norris House Inn is four blocks from the trail's King Street access. Go north on King two blocks and take a left on Loudoun Street. You'll see the Norris House on the left in a block and a half.

To reach Ivy Hall, take Old Route 7 (West Colonial Highway) through the center of Hamilton, turn left at South James Street, and in one block you'll see Ivy Hall straight ahead of you in the center of Burke Circle.

Key at-a-Glance Information

Length: 8 miles

Difficulty: Easy

Elevation gain: Gradual elevation gain leaving Leesburg

Scenery: Mostly pastoral

Exposure: Shady–65   Moderate–20   Exposed–15

Solitude: Busy on weekends

Surface: An eight-foot-wide asphalt lane runs parallel with a packed-dirt path. Hikers may take either.

Trail markings: Marked at intersections; asphalt trail is obvious

Author's hiking time: 3 hours

Season: All seasons

Access: No permits or fees

Maps: REI map or 64-page *Washington & Old Dominion Rail Trail Guide* both available at the W&OD Trail Office, 21293 Smiths Switch Road, Ashburn, VA 22011, or by calling (703) 729-0596

Other uses for trail: Cycling, horseback riding, rollerblading

Facilities: Food and toilet at Leesburg; snacks at Paeonian Springs and Hamilton

Shuttle: A morning bus takes passengers from Hamilton to Leesburg and returns from the east in the evening. Ivy Hall innkeepers will shuttle guests who make prior arrangements.

Lodging info:

The Norris House Inn, 108 Loudoun Street SW, Leesburg, Virginia; (703) 777-1806; (800) 644-1806; www.norrishouse.com; $$$$–$$$$$

Ivy Hall, 12 Burke Circle, Hamilton, Virginia; (540) 338-7426; $$$–$$$$

Alternative lodging:

None in Hamilton. For Leesburg, call the Loudoun County Visitor's Center, (800) 752-6118.

*The 45-mile Washington & Old Dominion is one
of the most popular rail-trails in the East.*

Warblers frequently build nests west of Leesburg between mile 36.5 and
the entrance to the 4-H fairgrounds near mile 37.3. Yellow-breasted chats
and common yellowthroats breed in denser areas along the trail. The
white-throated vireo is another common bird here, and wild turkeys are
regularly spotted just past the fairgrounds in spring. Grasshopper spar-
rows usually arrive in mid-May and breed in the open pastures on both
sides of the trail. A flock of bobolinks that migrate through the area during May can be seen and heard on the fences along a road that intersects
the trail north of milepost 36.5. Eastern kingbirds breed in that same area
and along Dry Mill Road to the west. The more rare loggerhead shrike
has been spotted west of the trail, again near milepost 36.5. Red-tailed,
red-shouldered, and Cooper's hawks also breed here.

Yellow-bellied sapsuckers usually winter along the trail, along with
hairy woodpeckers. The yellowish evening grosbeaks are regular fall
migrants through this area. You may even see some songbirds in Curry's

Landing, a wooded wayside with benches just south of King Street in Leesburg.

Pastoral scenery dominates the landscape after you leave Leesburg, making this the prettiest section of the trail. You pass some sprawling estates, a horse farm, ponds, and suburban homes interspersed with forest. Over the length of the trail, you can spot more than 400 species of wildflowers. In season, you're likely to see columbines, black-eyed Susans, betony, Queen Anne's lace, and Solomon's seal.

The trail curves along Dry Mill Branch after leaving Leesburg. After about four miles, the trail reaches its highest point at Clarks Gap on Catoctin Mountain. The trail crosses under and then over the historic Clarks Gap stone arch, passing over Route 7 and traveling beside Route 9 briefly. At milepost 39.5, the trail reaches the little village of Paeonian Springs, where you can walk out to a convenience store on the highway for a snack. This was originally a railroad rest stop, where passengers disembarked for a meal. From here, the trail runs along a high bank bordered by trees for another one and seven-tenths miles into Hamilton.

The old train station is still standing at Hamilton (milepost 41.2). Passenger service began with a steam train in 1859 and ended with diesel engines in 1951. The train stopped running in 1968, after years of failing to turn a profit. During its long life, the railway counted four United States presidents among its passengers: James Buchanan, Ulysses Grant, William McKinley, and Grover Cleveland, who liked to fish at Leesburg.

Hamilton, located seven miles from Leesburg, was once a thriving town that served as an Underground Railroad stop for slaves seeking freedom in the North. In a former era, residents of Washington took the train out to Sterling, Hamilton, or Bluemont to escape the summer heat of the city and enjoy the resorts along the rail line.

During the Civil War, John Mosby, known as the Grey Ghost, and his Confederate cavalry raiders made their headquarters in Hamilton. Although no major battles took place in the town, the Hamilton Raiders did skirmish with Union soldiers who came looking for them here.

A fire destroyed Hamilton's business district in 1926. Some residents count that fire as their good fortune because it stunted the town's development. Hamilton hasn't grown since then; it seems a town out of a different time among the burgeoning Washington suburbs, with no stoplights, no congestion, and little crime. Its first name of Harmony seems just as appropriate for the small town today.

Continue along the trail until mile 42.3 where you intersect with Ivandale Road (Route 709). The trail continues another two and seven-tenths miles to Purcellville, offering an optional hike of just under five and a half miles to and from the end of the Washington and Old Dominion Rail Trail. However, if you are ready to head toward your home away from home, turn left and walk until you reach Colonial Highway, then turn left and go two blocks to South James Street, and then turn right. In one block, you'll see Ivy Hall.

Norris House Inn
Leesburg, Virginia

Proprietors Pam and Don McMurray retired from fast-paced California corporate life to run an inn in a sleepy historic town, but they became so successful with their inn, tea room, and reception facility that they have little time to sit down. Maybe hard work is a habit for this couple, who publish a guide to the area's bike trails but haven't had time to ride the full length of even one.

Despite the McMurray's own pace, the 1760 inn in Leesburg's historic district radiates the charm and friendliness of an earlier era. Guests feel welcome to take tea in the sunroom, curl up with a book in front of the library fireplace, chat with other guests in the parlor, or stroll through the award-winning flower garden. Wine, iced tea, coffee, and lemonade are served evenings in the library.

The guest rooms are furnished in beautiful yet functional antiques. Some have canopy beds; some have brass beds; and some sport feather beds. Three rooms have working fireplaces, and all are air-conditioned. Tucked under the eaves on the third floor, my favorite, the Country Room, is awash in Shakerlike simplicity. The wood floor, walls, and ceiling are painted clean white and accented by a simple braided rug, cushioned window seats, and lace curtains. The view is so dominated by the Federalist houses that the sound of an automobile traveling over the brick street seems a startling anachronism.

The four-course breakfast begins with fruit and often ends with a sweet treat. Guests seated together in hourly servings often get to know each other as they did at colonial taverns.

Ivy Hall
Hamilton, Virginia

This 1881 Second Empire brick mansion is the only Loudoun County Victorian summer house still used as a residence and one of the few Richard Ruse structures not destroyed by Hamilton's 1926 fire. The wealthy Branch family members who built it were direct descendants of George Washington and loved such grand touches as two-story bay windows and wide center halls on each of the three floors.

The home's solid brick walls, interior as well as exterior, make it so soundproof that guests who crack open their windows are more likely to hear the owls and crickets than each other. To preserve the quiet atmosphere, Ivy Hall has no televisions.

The guest rooms, all located on the second floor, feature high ceilings, deep Victorian colors, antique furnishings, and queen-size beds. Two rooms have private baths, and one has a private porch overlooking the acre of lawn and garden.

Ivy Hall also offers a two-room suite for families or couples hiking together.

Breakfast is a several course affair, served in the restored dining room. Guests enjoy a typical breakfast of fruit, freshly baked bread or biscuits, and a gourmet main course of mushroom crepes in white wine sauce, quiche lorraine, or buttermilk pancakes with raspberry plum sauce. Hostess Georjan Overman also has compiled a repertoire of vegetarian and low-calorie dishes.

For the evening meal, guests often dine three blocks away at the unique Planet Wayside, open Wednesdays through Sundays.

Appendices

Walking Equipment Checklist

Shoes with good arch support, padded lining, and cushiony soles (tennis shoes are okay for rail-trails, but you may want hiking boots for the Appalachian and Allegheny Trails)

Hat

Daypack

Water (a quart every two hours is optimum in warm weather, if you won't be passing water sources in towns)

Lunch

Sunblock

Sunglasses

Insect repellent

Toilet paper

Map

Whistle

Identification

Paper money (some cabins and small B&Bs don't take credit cards)

Credit card

First aid kit containing Band-Aids, antibiotic ointment, aspirin or ibuprofen, antihistamine, and medication for bee sting

Light, waterproof jacket or poncho

Optional:
   Walking stick
   Binoculars
   Cell phone (ineffective in Pocahontas County section of Allegheny Trail)

Appendix B

Information

The following is a partial list of agencies, associations, and organizations to check with for information about the lands surrounding these hiking trails in Virginia and West Virginia.

American Hiking Society
P.O. Box 20160
Washington, DC 20041-2160
(703) 255-9304
www.outdoorlink.com

Appalachian Trail Conference
P.O. Box 807
Harpers Ferry, WV 25425
(304) 535-6331
www.atconf.org

Chesapeake and Ohio Canal National
Historical Park
P.O. Box 4
Sharpsburg, MD 21782
(301) 739-4200
www.nps.gov/choh/co_visit.htm

First Landing/Seashore State Park
2500 Shore Drive
Virginia Beach, VA 23451
(757) 481-2131
www.dcr.state.va.us/parks/1stland.htm

George Washington and Jefferson
National Forests
5162 Valleypointe Parkway
Roanoke, VA 24019
(540) 265-5100
www.southernregion.fs.fed.us/gwj

Greenbrier River Trail/Watoga State Park
Star Route 1, Box 252
Marlinton, WV 24954
(304) 799-4087
wvweb.com/www/greenbrier_rt.htm

Marion County WV Parks and Recreation
West Fork River Trail
316 Monroe St.
Fairmont, WV
(304) 363-7037
www.marioncvb.com

Monongahela National Forest
Greenbrier Ranger District

P.O. Box 67
Bartow, WV 24920-0067
(304) 456-3335
www.pocahontas.org

Mount Rogers National Recreation Area
3714 Highway 16
Marion, VA 24354
(540) 783-5196

North Bend Rail Trail
Route 1
Cairo, WV 26337
(304) 643-2391
www.wvparks.com/northbendrailtrail

New River Trail State Park
Route 2, Box 126F
Foster Falls, VA 24360
(540) 699-6778
www.dcr.state.va.us/parks/newriver.htm

Rails-to-Trails Conservancy
1400 Sixteenth Street NW
Suite 300
Washington, DC 20036
(202) 797-5400
www.railtrails.org

Shenandoah National Park
3655 US Highway East
Luray, VA 22835
(540) 999-3500
www.nps.gov/shen

Virginia Department of
Conservation and Recreation
203 Governor Street, Suite 302
Richmond, VA 23219
(804) 786-1712

Washington & Old Dominion Trail
c/o Northern Virginia
Regional Park Authority
5400 Ox Road
Fairfax Station, VA 22309
(703) 352-5900

Trails by Category

Paved trails

Huckleberry Trail in Montgomery County, Virginia
Washington and Old Dominion Trail in northern Virginia

Trails suited for mountain biking

Canaan Valley State Park to Blackwater Falls State Park, West Virginia
C&O Canal Towpath along Potomac
Greenbrier River Trail, eastern West Virginia
Hot Springs to Meadow Lane Lodge in Bath County, Virginia
Huckleberry Trail in Montgomery County, Virginia
New River Trail in southwest Virginia
North Bend Trail, north central West Virginia
Snowshoe Mountain Hut Hike, West Virginia
Virginia Beach: Bay to Grand Old Hotel
Virginia Creeper Trail in southwest Virginia
Washington & Old Dominion Trail in northern Virginia
West Fork River Trail, northern West Virginia

Trails suited for horseback riding

C&O Canal Towpath along the Potomac
Greenbrier River Trail in eastern West Virginia
Hot Springs to Meadow Lane Lodge in Bath County, Virginia
New River Trail in southwest Virginia
North Bend Trail in north central West Virginia
Virginia Creeper Trail in southwest Virginia
Washington & Old Dominion Trail in northern Virginia
West Fork River Trail in northern West Virginia

Rugged trails (lots of elevation gain and loss)

Allegheny Trail through eastern West Virginia
Appalachian Trail
Buena Vista's Elephant Mountain trails
Canaan Valley State Park to Blackwater Falls State Park, West Virginia
Hot Springs to Hidden Valley in Bath County, Virginia
Snowshoe Mountain, West Virginia
Wheezer Trail out of Narrows, Virginia

Rail-trails or towpath trails (relatively flat)

C&O Canal Towpath Trail
Chessie Trail in Lexington, Virginia
Greenbrier River Trail
Huckleberry Trail
New River Trail
North Bend Trail
Virginia Creeper Trail
Washington & Old Dominion Trail
West Fork River Trail

Hikes of 5 miles or less

Meadow Lane Lodge to Hidden Valley in Bath County, Virginia
North Bend Trail, North Bend State Park Lodge to Cairo
Snowshoe Mountain hut hiking

Hikes of 6–10 miles

Allegheny Trail, Cass to Green Bank
Appalachian Trail, Big Meadows to Skyland
Buena Vista, Virginia, trails up Elephant Mountain
Canaan Valley to Blackwater Falls
C&O Canal Towpath, Taylors Landing to Shepherdstown
Hot Springs to Meadow Lane Lodge
Huckleberry Trail
Lexington's Chessie Trail
New River Trail, Allisonia to Draper
Pearisburg to Narrows
Virginia Beach: Bay to Grand Old Hotel
Virginia Beach: Beach to Bay
Washington & Old Dominion Trail, Leesburg to Hamilton

Hikes of 11–15 miles

Allegheny Trail, Green Bank to Durbin
C&O Canal Towpath, Shepherdstown to Harpers Ferry
New River Trail, Galax to Fries Junction
North Bend Trail, Pennsboro to North Bend Lodge
North Bend Trail, Salem to West Union
North Bend Trail, West Union to Pennsboro
Virginia Creeper Trail, Green Cove to Damascus

Hikes of 15+ miles

Allegheny Trail, Cass to Durbin
Allegheny Trail, Huntersville to Cass
Greenbrier River Trail, Marlinton to Beard
Virginia Creeper Trail, Damascus to Abingdon
West Fork River Trail

Index

Ida Valley, VA, 89
Indian Gap Trail, Buena Vista, VA, 117, 119
Inns and hotels, Maryland
   Ground Squirrel Holler Bed and Breakfast, Sharpsburg, 37
Inns and hotels, Virginia
   Apple Tree Bed and Breakfast, Damascus, 163
   Asherowe, Lexington, 119–20
   Big Meadows Lodge, Shenandoah National Park, 90–91
   Buchanan Inn at Green Cove Station, Damascus, 168
   Budget Inn, Buena Vista, 120–21
   Budget Inn, Christiansburg, 94
   Buena Vista Motel, Buena Vista, 114
   Cavalier, Virginia Beach, 159–60
   Clay Corner Inn, Blacksburg, 99–100
   Claytor Lake Homestead Inn, Draper, 127–28
   Donaldson Brown Hotel, Blacksburg, 94
   Evergreen Bed and Breakfast, Christiansburg, 100–1
   Galax Motel, Galax, 132
   Green Cove Inn, Green Cove, 163
   Hidden Valley Bed and Breakfast, Warm Springs, 110–11
   Holiday Motor Lodge, Pearisburg, 140
   Homestead, Hot Springs, 109
   Ivy Hall, Hamilton, 177
   Knights Inn, Galax, 136
   L'Arche Bed and Breakfast, Blacksburg, 99
   Lazy Fox Inn, Damascus, 163
   Linda Lorraine's Bed and Breakfast, Pearisburg, 143–44
   Maples, Damascus, 163
   Meadow Lane Lodge, Warm Springs, 106–7, 109–10
   Mountain Laurel Inn, Damascus, 169
   New River Inn, Narrows, 144
   Norris House Inn, Leesburg, 176
   Oaks Victorian Inn, Christiansburg, 94
   Plaza Motel, Pearisburg, 140
   Ramada Plaza Resort Oceanfront, Virginia Beach, 150
   Rendezvous Motel, Pearisburg, 140
   Riversong Cabins, Fries, 136–37
   Silversmith Inn, Abingdon, 170
   Train Station, Allisonia, 128–29
   Virginia Beach Resort Hotel, Virginia Beach, 150–51, 158–59
   Williams Street Cabin, Galax, 135
Inns and hotels, West Virginia
   Acacia House, Fairmont, 80–81
   Bavarian Inn, Shepherdstown, 37–38
   Bellevue Bed and Breakfast, Shepherdstown, 32
   Blackwater Lodge, Davis, 29
   Briscoe House Bed and Breakfast, Harpers Ferry, 39
   Cannan Valley Resort, Davis, 28–29
   Carriage House Inn, Huntersville, 21–22
   Cheat Mountain Club, Durbin, 15–16
   Current Bed and Breakfast, Hillsboro, 47–48
   Elk River Inn, Slatyfork, 13–14, 22
   Gillum House, Shinnston, 81–82
   Graham's Motel, Marlinton, 42

About the Author

Su Clauson-Wicker lives with her husband Bruce in Blacksburg, Virginia, where she turns routine tasks such as banking and shopping into urban hikes. For the past 20 years, she's explored the Virginias on skis, by bicycle, and on foot. She holds two degrees: an undergraduate degree in developmental psychology from Cornell University and an M.S. in communication from Clarion University of Pennsylvania. Since graduation, she has had a diverse career as housemother in a children's home, educational television director, newspaper feature writer, editor of Virginia Tech Magazine, and costumed interpreter at the colonial Smithfield Plantation in Blacksburg.